Email: contact@2doubleccies.com

I0014650

Your CCNA Exam Success Strategy

The Non-Technical Guide Book

For
CCNA Routing and Switching

By

Dean Bahizad
CCIE 18887 (R&S, SP)

Vivek Tiwari
CCIE 18616 (R&S, SP)

Email: contact@2doubleccies.com

Copyright

Warranty and Disclaimer

Trademark Acknowledgments

Email: contact@2doubleccies.com

Praise for "Your CCNA EXAM Success Strategy"

Kenya Thomas , CCSI #34027

There are many books out there that describe the technical aspects of passing the CCNA, but there is nothing like "Your CCNA Exam Success Strategy". The first non-technical guide to passing the CCNA is extraordinary. From getting your family and kids on board, to selling the idea to your boss, to managing your energy. This book has it all. A non-technical personal guide written by two top notch Networking Experts. Buy it. Read it. Live it. And pass your CCNA!

Kojo Addae-Mintah   CCNP, CCSI #32929

"The co-authoring team of Vivek and Dean has once again delivered the missing piece of CCNA exam preparation. As a current CCNA instructor, I know the curriculum gaps that need to be filled to pass the CCNA exam. This clear concise guide fills those gaps and even gives relevant tips that all entry level engineers need to be successful in the Network Engineering field. "

Yash Modi,   CCNA, CCDA, CCNA Wireless, CCNP

"This book is a great mentor for someone who is preparing for CCNA. It highlights the practicality of the entire journey from preparation for the exam to all the hurdles one may encounter during the preparation course. A perfect guide one should follow as they prepare for the certification - a master piece."

Scott Butler CCIE#10560 CCAI (Cisco Certified Academy Instructor)

"Vivek and Dean have not only provided a great framework to get you to your target, but to keep you on track for reaching that target"

Nayyar Farooq, CCNA, MCSENET+, Security +, CISSP

"Gives in depth confidence, knowledge, encouragement, discipline and wisdom to pass the CCNA certification"

"An excellent addition to the collection of expertise, tips, and experiences and especially, those who are new in the field of information technology".

Maurice Walker, CCNA, CCNP

"It is a privilege and an honor to provide a review on a guide that will truly help the lives of many people obtain success in a career such as network engineering.

I would like to start by saying that this book is a very easy read. The chapters are short and to the point which is great. Each one tells a story which makes our own struggles easy to relate too.

I enjoy the ideas brought forth like having a mentor or a partner to work on things. It seems to do very well for you two. The chapter on setting a clear prize is one I'm going to start implementing. Usually I do have a little celebration after I pass a test but I love the idea of getting something concrete to remember my struggle and triumph. Most of these ideas are things I have incorporated into my routine over the past few years like talking with my spouse and using many different."

Glenn Sharpnack, CCIE Candidate

This book is the very first book a CCNA candidate should read during their preparation. Dean and Vivek give straight forward and easy to follow advice that will prepare you for success.

Email: contact@2doubleccies.com

What others are saying:

- ✓ *Everyone tells you to read a book. Vivek and Dean tell you how to read and pass the CCNA exam.*

- ✓ *The advice that is found in this book is not found in any CCNA book!*

- ✓ *This unique book covers the much needed non-technical aspects of CCNA exam preparation.*

- ✓ *Real mentorship from two CCIE's.*

- ✓ *With this book you never lose your way to becoming a CCNA.*

- ✓ *Enough guidance with built in flexibility for anyone who wants to be CCNA certified.*

- ✓ *Tells you how to study intelligently and not just study harder.*

- ✓ *They even tell you how to prepare your resume and how to interview.*

About The Authors

Vivek Tiwari   CCIE # 18616
(CCIE Routing and Switching and Service Provider)

Vivek Tiwari holds a Bachelor's degree in Physics, MBA and many certifications from multiple vendors including Cisco's CCIE. With double CCIE on R&S and SP track under his belt he mentors and coaches other engineers. Vivek has been working in Inter-networking industry for more than fifteen years, consulting for many Fortune 100 organizations. These include service providers, as well as multinational conglomerate corporations and the public sector. His five plus years of service with Cisco's Advanced Services has gained him the respect and admiration of colleagues and customers alike. His experience includes and not limited to network architecture, training, operations, management and customer relations; which made him a sought after coach and mentor, as well as a recognized leader.

He is also the author of

"Your CCIE Lab Success Strategy the non-Technical guidebook"

"Stratégie pour réussir votre Laboratoire de CCIE"

"Your CCNA Success Strategy Learning by Immersing – Sink or Swim"

Email: contact@2doubleccies.com

Bayan Dean Bahizad   CCIE # 18887 (R&S, SP)
CCNA, CCNP, CCDA, CCDP, CCSA, MCP, CIW Security Analyst, CEH, Infosec Professional, CISSP # 38843, Cisco IOS XR Specialist.

Dean Bahizad has a Bachelor of Applied Science (Engineering Honors) degree, and has been working with networks for more than fifteen years. His experience includes working on complex global networks as a Network Consulting Engineer for many fortune 100 companies. Dean has worked with financial institutions, automotive, manufacturing, and Service Provider segment. Dean has been with Cisco for the six plus years as a Consulting Engineer and Educational Specialist for both large enterprises and Service Providers. As an Educational Specialist, Dean has travelled around the globe in five continents and has worked closely with many Tier 1 Service Providers on training and deploying high-end equipment, such as CRS1/CRS3, CRS Multi-Chassis and ASR platform. Dean's talent is evident in his customer engagement, as the ability to deliver complex technologies in a simple, clear, and precise manner. If you have been in one of his classes you will know why people say you can laugh and learn at the same time. He is also the author of

"Your CCIE Lab Success Strategy the non-Technical guidebook"

"Stratégie pour réussir votre Laboratoire de CCIE"

Email: contact@2doubleccies.com

Acknowledgements

We would like to thank Donna Menna, our editor for converting our engineer-speak into an understandable and printable language.

We would also like to give a special thank you to Nandini Tiwari, Shiprali Tandon, Avantika Tiwari and Neeka Karimian for their help with the final editing.

We thankfully acknowledge the helpful review and suggestions from:

Kenya Thomas

Scott Butler

Kojo Addae-Mintah

Jeff Crooks

Glenn Sharpnack

Maurice Walker

Nayyar Farooq

Yash Modi

Lastly, we would like to thank everyone else who assisted and encouraged us with this work.

Email: contact@2doubleccies.com

Dedication:

Dean Bahizad: I would like to dedicate this book to my parents, my in-laws and my siblings who gave me so much to be thankful for. Your inspiration, teachings and blessings have been the invisible hand guiding me forward all my life.

Vivek Tiwari: I would like to dedicate this book to my parents who worked tirelessly and sacrificed so much to make me what I am today. They gave me the wings to fly and freedom to explore anytime, anyplace, anywhere.

Table of Contents

Email: contact@2doubleccies.com

INTRODUCTION

A Wiseman once asked, "Is there any greater blessing conceivable for a man than that he should become the cause of education, development, prosperity and honor of his fellow humans?" No, there is no other.

This book is written in order for you to become empowered and to understand what lies ahead for you in your CCNA journey.

To start off let us explain, what is CCNA? The Cisco Certified Network Associate (CCNA) is a Cisco certification, which tests you on the fundamentals of networking and is seen worldwide as one of the most popular and recognized networking certification. You may take one composite exam (single track) or two exams (ICND 1 & ICND2) to become a CCNA. We will cover these two options in more detail in chapters ahead, followed with a detailed timeline at the end of the book (Refer to chapter 37: Your flight plan). Nowadays it is a must for any network professional to hold at least one Associate Level certification track (CCNA) or more advanced certification such as Professional track Cisco Certified Network Professional (CCNP).

This certification not only proves your technical prowess but also adds prestige to your résumé. In many organizations, having a CCNA is a great way to build your knowledge to gain a better understanding of today's networks and to be recognized for your technical skills. **Your CCNA will inspire you to pursue a specialization** and may increase your salary and provide job security in today's volatile work environment. You may not know this; but CCNA certification has become harder to obtain in the past 10 years or so because certifications have to keep pace with the technology. If you really think about it, a large number of electronic devices that we touch are connected to the network. The cable channels on your TV, that credit card swipe at the gas pump/petrol pump, your smartphone, your laptop, ATM machine, and countless devices that we deal with are connected to the network. As a network engineer it is our job to provide these essential services without interruption to the end-user. The customer (end-user) may not be aware of the complex infrastructure behind communication of these devices, but they are keenly aware of the outages and the adverse impact on their daily lives.

Therefore, it is essential to know what services the network is providing to the society in general and how these devices communicate and exchange information via various protocols behind the scenes. The more we understand the communication and technology behind many of these devices, the more we appreciate it and the more we want to immerse ourselves in it.

When we were studying for our technical certification exams, we realized that all of the emphasis in preparation was on the technical aspects (which is of course is the aim of that certification) but an important element, the non-technical aspect was missing. There is an uncertainty about where to start and how to pass this test; **but most importantly, how to study effectively to gain sufficient knowledge so that you can use it in**

your daily work. This element has not been taught anywhere; until now. We have created this unique book to discuss the non-technical aspects of the CCNA exam. This book is for anyone, who is considering the CCNA challenge.

We want to tell you at the outset that we are engineers just like you, and because of that, this book is short and to the point. In our experience, we have seen many CCNA candidates approach the exam just like any other exam without proper strategies, planning or preparation. Due to the enormity of this exam, some get sidetracked or discouraged. In many instances, this is due to the non-technical aspects. Here are a few common scenarios that we have seen.

Scenario 1:

You plan and set a target date for scheduling your CCNA exam and start studying very hard. As you approach your target date, you realize that you are not fully prepared and so you postpone scheduling the CCNA exam. After doing this a couple of times you stop trying.

The problem in this scenario is that your target date is not planned well. Either the date is too aggressive or you are not able to devote the requisite amount of time for studying. Both of these are non-technical reasons that we will tackle in this book.

Scenario 2:

You start preparing after reading the CCNA Exam blueprint. The sheer number of books and video content on the internet can be overwhelming and at times confusing. When this happens, you may get overwhelmed and stop studying altogether.

The problem in this scenario is that you need to change the way you prepare and study. You need to be very specific about what training resources to use, and how to use them. This is another non-technical aspect. We will give you guidelines on how to maximize your studying efficiency later on in this book.

Scenario 3:

For your specific CCNA track you may purchase books and other training resources. The next question is, where do I start? Do I just read the first book and then move on to the next? When should I start my lab? Do I use simulators like DYNAMIPS/GNS3 or PACKET TRACER or should I buy actual gear? As you study you will see that the number of doubts in your mind start to grow. There comes a time when you have so many doubts and questions that you are overwhelmed. This may cause you to postpone or give up on your CCNA quest.

The problem in this scenario is that the candidate has many gaps in their knowledge. Without proper planning, preparation and mentoring, the technologies become more daunting. This book addresses the gradual step-by-step processes you should follow to succeed.

Scenario 4:

You have studied hard and are well prepared for your CCNA exam. You have scheduled your exam and you reach the testing center on time and complete all the formalities. You start your exam and you take your time with some of the multiple choice questions. You soon realize that with this speed, you may not be able to finish the exam on time. You start to speed up but are not sure of all the answers and your confidence and preparation is beginning to stall. You start to have doubts and think you will fail the exam.

The problem in this scenario is not your technical knowledge; it is the lack of a test taking strategy which is again a non-technical issue.

We can keep on going with many more scenarios; these and many other pitfalls are addressed in this book.

In this guidebook we tell you:

- The three essential keys to unlock your success.

- How to effectively utilize your training provider's resources.

- The four step process that will help when using Video on Demand.

- The Do's and Don'ts for your CCNA exam preparation.

- Detailed timelines with milestones to prepare for either the two exam CCNA approach or the single exam CCNA approach. (See Chapter 4 to decide which approach is suitable to you)

- How you can do all of this, and still work your full time job.

This book is easy to follow. What we have written is advice that we gave to others about our Cisco certification experiences. It contains short concise chapters that will not take away your study time, it should only enhance it.

All the chapters in this book are suggestions based on our successful personal experiences. Use these suggestions to suit your specific needs. But **remember, these are suggestions, and not rules that are set in stone** to help you succeed in your CCNA exam.

If you have a huge task which is outside your comfort zone, you need to break it down into smaller manageable chunks. At times, you may feel overwhelmed, but you need to be in control and rationalize the purpose behind this undertaking. This reminds us of a story someone told us, about a man who was planning to follow his dream of hiking the entire Appalachian Trail in one summer. For those who don't know the Appalachian Trail is about 2,184 miles (3515 KM) and passes through 14 states on the eastern side of US. He knew very well that many enthusiasts start to hike the trail in one season but can't complete. He was excited for the challenge and to experience what so many people start but only few get to finish. He had planned that each day he will hike the trail from 15 to 20 miles and next day he will get up and do the same regardless, rain or shine he will move until he reaches the end. Once he started he realized how difficult it was. The difference in terrain, weather, and elevation made it difficult to do the 20 miles a day. After just 10 days he was on the verge of quitting but then told himself if he quits now he will think of himself as a quitter all his life. Instead of thinking about the difficulties and the long walk he told himself that all he has to do is put one foot in front of the other, while looking at the nice views around him. Before long the day was done and he was closer to his ultimate goal. He continued to do this and soon realized that his goal was much closer and achievable.

Once you follow our guidelines and decide on what path to take, your sole job is to be persistent and aggressively pursue your plan, without looking at the distance that you have traveled or the long road ahead, just keep going.

We recognize that CCNA is at least four to an eight month project (depending on your skill set and the time you can allocate for studying) that you need to break down into daily, weekly activities and goals. Thus the question that you should be asking yourself is, "**What can I do in the next fifteen minutes to help with my daily goal?**" This question changes the way you look at things, namely breaking down CCNA into daily, weekly tasks. The goal is to get a CCNA, but what you need to realize is that every fifteen minutes counts and can **bring you one step closer to achieving your goal**.

This guidebook will give you an inside view of CCNA Exam preparation. We will be mentoring you through a step-by-step process and provide answers to the questions you will have on your journey to this demanding certification. Some ideas in this book may sound deceivingly simple, yet they will make a huge difference once you implement them. For example, it is important that before you go to bed; you spend five minutes of your time reflecting on what you did for that day and write down your plan for the next day. This simple gesture will prepare you for the next day to hit the ground running. You will not waste a single minute thinking about what you should study or where you should start.

We are here to give you the **straightforward, no-nonsense picture of what it will take to get your CCNA.** These strategies have worked for us, and we are confident that they will help you in your endeavor too.

Visit our website at **2doubleccies.com** for additional information.

CHAPTER 1: ARE YOU READY TO BE EARN YOUR WINGS?

Do you really want to be a CCNA?

Since you are reading this, you are obviously considering the CCNA exam. In writing this book, we wanted to inform you what to expect in the simplest terms. No sugarcoating. No exaggeration. This is a frank conversation from one engineer to another.

When talking to other engineers about CCNA—whether it is those who have obtained it, or those who have failed to obtain it, or even those who have just considered obtaining it—you invariably hear some or all of the following comments:

1. It is a lot of work.

2. CCNA certification is not worth the time and money it takes to earn it. (Not true)

3. When studying for the CCNA exam, 24 hours a day doesn't seem like nearly enough time.

4. You must focus on CCNA and nothing else.

5. You must be rich to take the CCNA exam because it is expensive.

6. The CCNA exam is very difficult and designed for you to fail.

7. Only those who read the exam dumps pass the CCNA exam.

8. I failed my exam because the test evaluation is flawed.

9. The only way to pass is to know the "Correct Cisco Answer".

Are all of these comments true? Of course not; some of the above statements are made by individuals to justify why they are not CCNA's. Obtaining a CCNA is definitely a formidable task, requiring many hours of study and sacrifice over an extended period of time (at least four to eight months). In spite of that, do you still want to be a CCNA? If your answer is "yes", ask yourself why? Ask yourself that, then list at least the top five reasons in the space we have provided. Take it from us it is important that you list at least five reasons. If you can think of more, list them as well. Take out a piece of paper, if you need to. This list will help you isolate your reasons, and even solidify them in your own mind. Because there will be times where you feel discouraged, or lose focus, or wonder why you are working so hard. In those instances, you can return to **this list to remind yourself** of the benefits.

My Top-Five Reasons for Becoming a CCNA

1. _____

2. _____

3. _____

4. _____

5. _____

Those who have become CCNA's agree that the exam takes a lot of work and a serious commitment, but they also agree that the results are

worth it. When talking to them, they may describe some of the difficulties they encountered, but they will also explain how they were able to work at it and persevere. They are proud of their achievement, and if you were to ask them **"what are the most important qualities a successful candidate must possess", they will almost invariably say a positive attitude and an unwavering commitment.**

CHAPTER 2: A TALE OF FOUR ENGINEERS

Before we delve any deeper into this book, we want to tell you true stories about four engineers we know. To protect their identities, we have changed a few personal references and altered events slightly.

Joe Engineer 1: About 45 years old, with 20 plus years of work experience in Networking/IT

Kevin Engineer 2: About 33 years old, with 8 years of experience in Telecom.

Jeff Engineer 3: About 25 years old, with 2 years of part time Networking Experience.

Christine Engineer 4: About 30 years with 5 years' of mixed telecom plus network experience.

Joe (Engineer 1) works for a large automotive manufacturing company; he had worked in the networking industry for many years and has the experience.   As part of his annual performance review with his manager, Joe is being asked to get CCNA certified to show his ranking with his peers and new hires alike. He has quite a bit of experience and decides to take the exam right away. He did not pass and realized that CCNA requires well rounded knowledge in many aspects of networking. Instead of reading and understanding the technical topics he decided to study the brain dumps and after few months of studying with on and off preparation he attempts the exam.   On this attempt he fails by a few points. Discouraged he postpones this goal for a few months. Well, those few months turned into years. With all the personal, relationship and work commitments; consideration for CCNA became a monumental task. Joe always had a reason why he could not study, for example, "My daughter will be graduating in a few years from high school and I want to spend more time with her", "I am taking the entire family to the Grand Canyon", or "We are going camping for the next two weeks" or "This is hunting season and I can't focus during this time"; or best of all, "These dumps have too many questions and I can't memorize them all". Still to this day, Joe has his reasons why he can't get certified. With this approach where is Joe today? Can you guess?

Kevin (Engineer 2) a single father who works the late night shift with a tier three local service provider. As a junior engineer he has worked for many hours on most of the issues and has jumped into any project that the management team assigned him. He comes to a class which is for Cisco equipment used by that Service provider. In that class although he is the junior engineer compared to the other students, he brings in so much energy that his presence is noticed as soon as he walks into the classroom. He came there to learn. He asked questions that he could not find the answers to and he stayed after the class to get more clarification and a chance to do a whiteboard session with the instructor. He clearly loved technology and after talking to the instructor decided to do CCNA. He studied hard and with such enthusiasm he went to the exam. He was ready, prepared and confident that he would pass. Well, after the test was finished, the score card showed that he had failed. He decided that he would not give up; he scheduled his second attempt. For the next two months, he came up with a study plan and submitted his request to his boss to use the company education budget to partially pay for his CCNA boot camp. Kevin loved to be challenged and loved the technology. He went to the boot camp with total focus to pass the next round regardless of how many hours of studying it took; can you guess where Kevin is now?

Jeff (Engineer 3) is just 2 years out of college. He was interested in networking and worked hard to learn and understand the concepts. While studying for his Bachelors in computer science he also started working part time on the college network. He was highly recommended by his professor and was ready to work nights or odd hours to make changes on the network. With a little push from his peers he started studying for CCNA. He got the books from the library to see if it was something that he can do. He loved it, and to the amazement of his peers, was a CCNA in about five months. His experience with the college network and CCNA landed him a better paying job at a local company. Five years later where is he now?

Christine (Engineer 4) was an automotive company employee who dropped out of college and started working for them because of sheer family needs but that burning desire to complete her college education was always there. She started with general office work and soon discovered that she was good with the PBX and telephone system. She soon started helping the telecom team and jumped at the opportunity of learning all about Voice over IP (VoIP) when the company went for this new technology. After a total of 5 years with the company she was laid off. This was a big setback for her but also a blessing because now she was able to enroll herself at the local community college under the company's continuing education program which was a part of the layoff package. The local community college was offering a Cisco academy program which would give her a solid IT background and specialization in networking in two years. Her heart was set to get the job done and her mind conscious of the task ahead. She also realized that this field has few women engineers and there were companies with incentives to hire women. She took the Cisco academy path with the intention to get her degree along with Cisco certification credentials. It took her two years to study. Where do you think Christine is now?

I am sure you are curious where are these engineers today?

Joe Engineer 1: Was sent to the Network Operation Center for level 1 support where he is still working as the first line of support and talks about the good old days.

Kevin Engineer 2: Got his CCNA and did some more specialized courses specific to the service provider equipment and is a level 2 engineer.

Jeff Engineer 3: Has the most dramatic story here. He is now a Cisco employee with a CCIE all within a few years.

Christine Engineer 4: After finishing her degree Christine got married and has moved to the tech valley and is working as a Network Engineer.

All of these engineers were intelligent, talented and decided that they wanted to make a difference in their lives. All of these folks reached their CCNA certified status and moved to their professional tracks except Joe who was reluctant to attend the classes and gave up. Therefore, it is important to realize that to make a difference in your life you have to **recognize the changes and challenges and overcome them** in order to get to your destination. At one time or the other, we all have heard quotes that are similar to the following

- The more difficulties one sees in the world the more perfect one becomes.

- The more you plough and dig the ground the more fertile it becomes.

- The more you put the gold in the fire the purer it becomes.

- The more you sharpen the steel by grinding the better it cuts.

Therefore the more challenges one faces the more perfect one becomes." These quotes sum up the situation in a very precise manner telling us that difficulties are part of the process and if you choose to continue on this path you need to accept and expect them.

Perhaps you would say that someone will be able to identify the four mentioned engineers by our descriptions. Unfortunately, this could not be farther from the truth. Stories like these are all too common. We have seen it, and many variations of it, many times over the years. That is why we wanted to write this book. We wanted to help you avoid some of the common obstacles in achieving your goal. This book is the distillation of many years of experience, ours and of our colleagues— both men and women with many different skill sets, study habits, and from many different countries—and we hope that you will learn as much from it as you will from any technical book that you may have purchased.

CHAPTER 3: WHY THIS GUIDEBOOK

This book will enable you to get yourself the CCNA certified status and help you plan to move ahead in your career.

As an instructor, I $^{(Dean)}$ have taught many engineers who were keenly interested in one certification or the other. Some did not pass the certification exam in spite of their best intentions because of the non-technical obstacles. Certification exams can be very intimidating for some engineers, so intimidating that they could not sleep the night before, even though they knew the technologies. Others had no strategy for study and preparation for the exam. Some of them treated this like any other exam that they could pass by just studying for a day or two before the exam. All this resulted in them not passing the exam.

By listening to their experiences, both authors (Vivek and Dean) realized that many of the issues they described were non-technical, and perhaps lacked strategy. We therefore decided to provide a comprehensive, and easy to read guidebook that would cover all these issues and provide the answers and the approach that we feel would overcome the above mentioned and many other obstacles. In our experience, **we noticed that the non-technical side of the CCNA exam is just as important as the technical side.** Whenever we are asked about our certification experience, we talk about the technical and the non-technical aspects. Almost invariably, the non-technical aspects are valued more. While studying for our own certifications as well as talking to, tutoring, and inspiring many other candidates in their quest for certifications, we realized that there were very few, if any, resources for this information. This is one of the only books (to our knowledge) that fills that non-technical gap for CCNA certification.

However, we also realize that each individual has a different approach to learning. We are simply writing about what worked for us and what resonated most with our fellow engineers. We encourage you to adapt this text to best suit your needs and style of learning. **Consider this more of a guidebook than an infallible set of rules to follow.** For instance, from our experience and interviews with a number of other certified engineers, we suggest that after the basic background work, you should be able to attain your CCNA within four to eight months (See Chapter 37: Your flight plan). Our suggestion of eight months does not mean that if you complete your CCNA in twelve months you are underperforming. This also does not mean that you cannot do it in less than four months. This timeline is a framework that can be used to make your own study schedule that is best suited for your situation and needs.

CHAPTER 4: ONE STOP OR NON-STOP FLIGHT

Should I take one exam or two exams

One of the most asked questions by candidates are which exam track should I follow for the CCNA? Meaning, do I take a dual course path with ICND1 and ICND2 or should I take one big leap with single composite CCNA exam? The answer to this depends on your situation. Let's examine this:

A. If you are new to this industry (someone with no IT background), who wants to do CCNA because you are interested in networking, and want to choose that as your career, then we advise you to take the two exam approaches. Our advice is for you to earn your stripes and really learn the technology. We have created two detailed timelines for the dual exam track and based on your background you may choose the best timeline that suits your needs and your abilities.   In brief, as someone who is coming into the networking field you may find taking two exams a more attractive option. This path would give more time on each technology; therefore you will learn and absorb the details of networking. These details are essential to give you a solid foundation for your career.

B.   We recommend the single exam track for those who have been working in telecom industry with network devices or have experience with networking such as being a Server

Administrator. With this kind of experience and having the fundamentals of networking down pat you may find the composite exam a more attractive option for yourself. You should be ready to devote a significant amount of time to studying. If you can do that and follow one of our timelines at the end of the book, you should be able to pass the composite exam.

C. **An exception** we have seen is that there are engineers who do not have any background in networking but start studying and pass the single exam in record breaking time. This seemed amazing to us but when we looked deeper we found that these engineers were surely exceptional. I am not talking about being exceptionally intelligent. They are surely intelligent but they have an exceptional commitment and possess the ability to sit down for twelve to fourteen hours straight on the weekend to study and grasp new information. They also have great mentors close by (a brother, a neighbor or someone at work). This combination of total devotion, immediate help and time commitment helps shape them into a successful engineer very fast. However this is something that we do not see on a day to day basis but we surely want you to be aware of it.

Regardless, of taking CCNA in composite exam or dual exam, **the goal is not just having the certification, but also having the knowledge base and sufficient hands on experience to deal with issues in the production network and to add value to the networking team.** The exam's financial cost should not be a factor, since it is the same whether you take the composite exam (Single exam track) or two separate exams (Dual exam track). However, the time taken to achieve your certified status is a factor. You are the best judge of your situation.   This book gives you the tools to prepare you for the technical side (Chapter: 34 Do's, Chapter 35: Don'ts and Chapter 37: Your flight plan) and the non-technical side (all other chapters). Armed with this knowledge you should be able to make a very informed and confident decision about which path to take to move ahead.

CHAPTER 5: CCNA CAREER PATH

It's annual review time and the company is downsizing. You are asked to get your CCNA to qualify for a networking position. You may be new in the networking field, but you have many years of IT experience in related fields like Server Administration or Racking, Stacking and putting base configuration templates on equipment or even coding protocols. Your first reaction is to ask your colleagues Jack and Lisa to tell you what to do.

One option is to take the exam dump and memorize questions and answers. Many say that within a few weeks you can get your CCNA. But are you comfortable to take on the network and all its complex protocols by yourself with just a paper certification and no learned knowledge? The second option is to tell your boss that you are going to take X number of months (our timeline at the end of the book may help) and prepare a strategy in order to learn the protocols and technologies and to be a reliable source for your team and entire networking department.

For military service men or women who may already have played around with the networking gear, there are programs by Cisco and others designed to pull you through the entire certification quickly. It is up to you to do your own research and find out what options are available to you and visit the link below;

https://learningnetwork.cisco.com/community/careers/career_development/student

For a Technical Project Manager (PMP), you need to have your CCNA so you can make sense of the conversation or assign tasks to engineers with the proper skills. Many companies have their sales force and the Project Managers (PM) to take the CCNA certification to bring added value to the team. This helps them explain the issues to the customer and executives alike in a manner that can be understood. Having the fundamental networking knowledge make the projects more successful as you are aware of any issues and understand the downfalls compared to the Project Manager without any technical background.

For college students, there are many career path options available with partner programs where they recruit you right out of college and provide training with a contract (check Cisco's website for more information).

For internship programs, many colleges provide you with the means to penetrate the job market and breakthrough the barriers. You will get to work with professionals and learn the skills that you need to take on responsibilities. Some programs treat their interns as part of their team and may provide them with some of the same perks as employees; for example training sessions, free parking, employee development etc. Once you prove yourself as a worthy member to the team and the department, odds are that they will call you in the next term of internship and many times will have a position available for you upon your graduation.

Cisco has some programs as well, for example the Associated Program where you can become an Associate System Engineer (A-SE) part of the

Sales force, Associate Network Consulting Engineer (A-NCE) part of post sales, Associate Project Manager (A-PM) and others alike. So the next logical question is how do I get into these programs? If you are a graduate with good grades, company recruiters usually have a presence on campus either via a co-op program or other career services that the school/college provides. Reach out to those departments and make appointments with the career counselor. Have them help you polish your resume, your interview skills and find out about student job fairs and other activities and networking opportunities within your school. **You may need to build a relationship** with these folks and once you have contacts for companies of your choice **continue networking and building a bond** that would be beneficial for both of you. Since this may take some time, you need to look into these programs as soon as you start school/college.

The associate programs that we have mentioned above can start you up with a good salary, benefits, and may move you to the company campus for a few weeks or months, providing full amenities and training classes. The graduates of these programs will have gained the experience of an engineer with four to five years of experience, within a few months. The company invests in you so that they may benefit from a skillful and talented employee who would commit to them and their cause for a certain period stated in the contract and potentially even longer. Think about it; you are getting paid to be trained all expenses paid and a guaranteed job. This is an opportunity many would grab in a heartbeat.

These programs are designed so that you can get your CCNA/CCNP completed and are on your way towards your CCIE. This is especially possible through the A-SE and A-NCE program.

Since the company pays for your expenses, there are some expectations or even contracts that you have to sign prior to joining these programs. The contract usually states how long you are committed to work for that company. Again these factors depend on the hiring companies and their policies. Please check the company website for more details.

For those professionals who seek to boost their careers and have already gained a few years of networking experience, there are professional programs which could also be of interest. These programs last about three to six months depending on the company. They produce the same results as the associate program, but they skip through some of the basic fundamentals because you should already be well versed in those.

Once again in all of these instances, **it is up to you to thoroughly research and find the program that will benefit you.** Here are two great websites that will connect you to jobs that need Cisco certification.

www.ciscopartnertalentnetwork.com

www.partnertalentevents.com

CHAPTER 6: HOW DIFFICULT IS IT?

It is difficult but not impossible?

CCNA can be a difficult certification depending on your past experience and how much you know about Cisco IOS and Cisco technologies and how to practically implement it.

You may be asking yourself, what is Cisco IOS?

Cisco IOS is the code that runs on all of Cisco routers and switches (except for the higher end routers and Datacenter platforms that may run IOS-XR, NX-OS or SAN-OS). You need to become very familiar with that. It's like learning a new language which you may struggle with at first, but once you immerse yourself, it is second nature. The analogy of language is realistic, as different vendors have adopted different operating systems, syntax and logic of configuring the equipment; nevertheless, all of these devices are providing the same functionality from OSI model perspective namely (layer 1-4). For example configuring the network address on a Linux Server, a Windows Server and a Cisco router might have different syntax (speaking different languages) but the end result is that these devices are able to connect to the network.

Initially learning the IOS may seem difficult especially for those of us who are used to a GUI (graphical user interface) based driven operating system. As you get more hands-on experience and practice, it becomes easier. For example, you may be wondering what is EIGRP, OSPF, NAT? What are they used for? How is it relevant to my everyday life and to others? How do I configure a device for these protocols? How do I troubleshoot these protocols using Command Line Interface (CLI) commands?

CLI is a tree structure format, with certain rules you can configure an IOS device. For most network engineers **CLI is the way** to configure most of the routers, switches and other Cisco devices like firewalls.

As you start reading and learning about protocols like OSPF, EIGRP, HSRP, **you will realize how these communicate, their importance and the role they play to bring all the end-devices together transparently.** You can think of these protocols independently but they have true dependency amongst themselves based on their role. For example, think of an automotive assembly plant. Though there are thousands of employees, each is assigned a particular task, like putting the windshield, attaching the doors, putting seats, attaching the engine and others, etc. When you combine each task in a specific logical order, the end results would be a fully functional drivable automobile.

In the field of networking, each protocol is designed to solve a specific problem or issue and once you design a network using these protocols, the result would be a functional network that uses many protocols to serve a particular purpose. Let me give you two examples.

Bank ATMs: If you are designing a network for ATMs, you will see that there is very little information transferred for each transaction (account number, pin and a few more details). Data has to be transmitted with absolute reliability and has to be encrypted. Can you imagine that money is deducted from your account but the commands to the ATM machine to dispense money are lost in transit? That would be unacceptable. Similarly, you do not want anyone to tap the wire, get your ATM card, and pin information. That is the reason for encryption. Although encryption adds a slight delay but that is absolutely acceptable to you in this case.

The 4G Cellphone network: The Fourth Generation (4G) or Long Term Evolution (LTE) phone system has to provide you with a high-speed data and voice link even when you are moving and connect you from the closest cell tower to the Mobile Switching Center (MSC). Think of MSC as a central office of all mobile communications. In a large metropolitan area such as Chicago there may be a handful of these per carrier. When the end user tries to make a phone call from their mobile phone to another mobile phone; it would trigger a chain reaction that would start from one user to the cell tower, to the MSC, perhaps across the planet to another MSC in another country down to the cell tower of the remote user. All of these events happen extremely fast and seamless to the users, which is exactly how it should be.

The network design for the above two situations is different as it serves a different need and purpose. Speed is of the essence here so encryption is not done. You may have realized by now that as the use of the network grows to serve more and more of our needs, a variety of protocols have been made to serve these needs.

All these protocols, like an individual person on the auto assembly line are doing their own job but have to be dependent on others to make that ATM transaction successful or that Cell phone connection to work.

Once you understand the fundamental concepts behind each of the protocols, and how these interact with each other and practice them by configuring, running show commands and debugs you will be able to connect the dots and see the picture clearly. But, you need to work on it, as it will take time effort and perseverance to reach this level of understanding.

In general your endeavor may take at least four to eight months to really understand the concepts then start applying them by doing hands on labs and eventually passing the CCNA exam.

Another factor to keep in mind is that as you study, **you may want to read some of the best practices whitepapers written by Cisco engineers** and other engineers as well as your company's best practices. This would really open your eyes as to why things are done a particular way in your organization.

We wanted to add a word of caution here for the exam. Please remember that just because you know the best practices and use it in a production network, it does not mean that this would be the best for another network. (Think of the examples of the ATM and cell phone network. Traffic from the ATM to the bank needs to have high quality encryption while that from the cell phone to MSC does not need any encryption). Similarly those best practices might not have been kept in mind when framing the CCNA exam questions or CCNA lab questions. When unsure in the interpretation of the question, re-read the question, look at the possible answers in case of multiple-choices. Perhaps one or two of the four to five choices could be eliminated immediately.

To sum it all up, you have a lot to cover. So tighten your seat belt and get ready to devote your time and energy to this certification along with your full and complete commitment.

What Would We Do

We both understood early on that CCNA certification is not to be taken lightly. This is because you not only have to understand the concept, but you also have to know how to configure, deploy and troubleshoot the network. For example we all know that reading a book on how to play a piano and playing the piano are completely different. While reading the book gives you the knowledge it is the practice that makes you play it. Doing CCNA is like reading the book on playing the piano, practicing to play it and also knowing how to fine tune it.

Besides reading about the technologies we would spend a lot of time on hands on implementation of technologies. Every time we made a network with specific configurations work, we felt a great sense of joy. This proud feeling is what drove us further and made us work longer and harder.

One of our strategies would be to take a job or a role that enables you to implement what you have learnt. For example if you start working in a Network Operations Center you will handle the first level of calls and will soon know about the types of problems that happen on a network and how these are handled. What basic information is needed for troubleshooting and how you can get assistance from Cisco? On the other hand if you start working for a network integrator you will be doing a lot of hands on work with cables, SFP's, different types of fibers and their connectors, physical installs and configurations.

The key here is to take on as much as you can comfortably and do it completely. If you don't understand something ask around. Your colleagues know that you don't know everything but when you show that urge to learn and move ahead they will help you.

CHAPTER 7: INVESTING IN YOURSELF

Invest in your CCNA Certification

As you may already know, both of us hold many certifications from multiple vendors. Being CCIE certified means that we dedicated an enormous amount of time, effort, and money into our career. We strongly believe that we need to spend a percentage of our salaries into continuous education and self-improvement; and certification is a great avenue to consider.

In an interview, we were asked why we spend so much time and money on certifications. For us that seemed like a wrong question to ask; instead, we should be asking why we spend a significant amount of time and money on other things in our lives, such as entertainment. It is surprising that we spend many hours on activities like going to movies, sporting events, computer games, PPV, and social networks. For example it's very typical for us to watch TV for hours, but we may not even know it. During one of my [Dean] travels, I was staying with a family friend and the TV was on for most of the day, (every time I arrived or left the TV was on and they were in front of it). I asked my friend, how they could watch so much TV. He objected and explained that he barely watches any TV and he only watched three or four hours of news related programs.

The point for them and others is that **we think of our wants as necessities in our lives.** Without noticing, we spend time and money on items that may not bring direct results or changes to our lives.

Entertainment, baseball games and social networks have a place in our lives but these should not impede self-development. We believe, by improving one self, we can allow for the betterment of ourselves, our families, and our world.

The choices that you made earlier have gotten you where you are today. **The decisions that you make today will change your life tomorrow;** choose CCNA so your future will be richer and brighter than your past and present.

We have no doubt in our mind that CCNA certification can give you the creditability and recognition for what you know in the networking area.

We admire your decision to take the CCNA certification challenge and reading this book.

Just like any company that invests in their future by making new products and marketing their line of products, we have to do the same. We have to continuously build our skill set to keep abreast with the newer technologies and keep ourselves marketable in this competitive job market.

You should also make it your mission to find out your company's policy concerning elite certification programs. Many companies (Cisco, its partners particularly and Service Providers) offer financial assistance for technical courses like CCNA and also subsidize or pay for books and the exam costs. It's up to you to find out which, if any, your company provides. You may have to make a case to your company as to why they should invest their money into your enterprise. In these instances, you should outline all the benefits the company will see by having a certified person on staff. Be sure to have your manager advocate your case to his or her superiors.

Explore all avenues. Often, there are many hidden resources and policies within any organization that you may not even be aware of. Check the continuing education budget to see if certification falls within that category or subcategory. Talk to your manager and your HR manager and find out what's available. Remember, the squeaky wheel gets the grease. Make your intentions known.

Many large companies, Cisco partners, and educational training partners are required to have Cisco Certified staff. This means that the demand for CCNAs is great, and so is the potential that one of them will sponsor your efforts.

Another resource for getting your company to help you in your learning is Cisco Learning Credits. Whenever a large purchase is made from Cisco, learning credits is usually a part of it as Cisco wants to make sure that the customer purchasing the hardware can train their staff. Talk to your manager or local Cisco Sales team to learn more about these learning credits. There may already be some there for you to use.

If you are working for a Cisco partner, there is a lot of training available from Cisco on the Cisco Partners website. Some of this training is for cutting edge products and you should make full use of these if you have access to it.

A good friend told me years ago that you have to start looking at certification as a business and sell it as such. If you do it right, you may receive not just all of the expenses incurred, but also time off for studying, travel costs, and even company rewards and a recognition letter to you and your department executive.

Based on some of the salary surveys and the people that we interviewed, many CCNA's make more money than their counter parts without any certification. Furthermore, based on our experience and years of service, many CCNA engineers can make from 45 - 65 thousand dollars with overtime in the U.S.

When we say invest, we really mean it, because it is truly a beneficial investment. As you put money into certification, you should know that it will pay you many times; even better than the stock market. Once you get into the networking field, you will go from CCNA (> 50K Salary) to the specialist certification (>60K Salary) and then to professional certification for example CCNP (>80K Salary) and then the expert level certification a CCIE (>100K Salary) in a span of 5 to 6 years. If you work hard and truly understand networking and move up the certification level, you will see your rewards become greater and greater. I do not mean just money when I talk about the rewards. I also mean the respect from your peers and management, and the job satisfaction that you get by maintaining and upgrading your organizations network.

Once you have CCNA under your belt you can choose which branches of networking interest you more; voice, security, service provider, data center, wireless, video or any other field. For a majority of these, there is a professional and expert level track which you can pursue.

What We Do

Both of us invest a percentage of our time and salaries for continuous improvement in our skills. This could be in the form of :

- Purchasing books

- Attending online webinars

- Reading documents and journals

- Meeting experts in newer technologies or taking these experts out for a lunch/dinner to have quality one on one time with them

- Going to local networking events

- Attending formal training courses.

- Find a mentor amongst our colleagues, friends or online using our guidelines in Chapter 19: The Air traffic Controller.

CHAPTER 8: RESOURCES & BUDGET, METHODS & STRATEGIES

Below is a short list of expenses you should keep in mind while making your decision on whether or not to pursue your CCNA (when estimating the costs).

1. CCNA training resources, such as Video on Demand and/or Audio on Demand

2. Instructor-led classes or boot camps

3. CCNA examination fees

4. CCNA related reference books / e-books

5. CCNA simulation hardware

6. CCNA simulation software (many free version are available).

7. Actual Cisco hardware.

8. Taking time off for studies and the actual exam.

This list is by no means comprehensive. Consider it a rough guide to the overall expenses you can expect. Feel free to add or subtract items according to your situation and expectations. The good news is that CCNA is one certification many companies are willing to pay for, at least in part.

When planning financially for your CCNA exam, plan for at least two attempts. I'm not saying this to discourage you, but because failure on the first or second attempt is all too common and we don't want you to have to abandon all of your hard work and sacrifices due to financial issues.

The good thing about investing in a variety of resources is that many can be used for future training. For example, the powerful PC or laptop that you purchased for network simulation can be used to simulate networks for your CCNP preparation also. The study habits and learning capacity you develop for CCNA can easily be used for your next certification. The books you purchase will be a good reference for you. Another approach to achieve the CCNA certification is to take Cisco academy courses where they are available.

Overall, the time and money invested in CCNA will be paying you many times over in the future. It is up to you to utilize this investment.

What Would We Do

When I [(Vivek)] did my CCNA, I ended up buying my own books but managed to convince my employer to pay for my exam fee. They agreed to pay it if I passed the exam. If I were taking my exam now, I would leverage the local library first. There are many good books on networking and CCNA available in the library these days. I would also ask my friends and colleagues if they have their CCNA books lying around. Once I start reading and am sure that I will invest the time to read and take the CCNA exam, I would talk to my Supervisor or Manager and ask them if they can help me in my CCNA quest. However when I ask them, it would be very specific and precise. Instead of asking, "I need help with the CCNA exam", I would ask, "I have decided to increase my knowledge by achieving CCNA certification. It is going to cost me X amount dollars for books and X dollars for the exam. It is going to take X number of months. I wanted to know if the company can help in this endeavor." I would add further that the company can not only help me financially but can also help me by giving me some paid time off exclusively for studying. The precise time and dollar amount tells my manager that I have given this a lot of thought and not only that I am serious about it but I have planned this. This also gives my manager the exact scope of my requests and he/she can easily come up with a decision very soon.

I would also ask my manager to use spares and older network devices to setup my own lab at work.

CHAPTER 9: WHAT TO EXPECT WHEN YOU EARN YOUR WINGS?

What happens when you get your CCNA?

You will remember those moments clearly when you were sitting at your CCNA exam test center and after answering all the questions to the best of your knowledge you gave one final click of the mouse to the last question and then you had to wait. Although this wait was for only a few seconds, those few seconds felt like an eternity. And then you saw PASSED flash up on the screen. It is a euphoric moment. You can hardly contain yourself. You are happy and smiling as you step out of the exam room. There is a rush of happiness all around. Once you get the printout of your score you just see the overall great score you had. Now you can inform your family and close friends who have helped all along about your success. A few hours later you are still in a celebratory mood and why not? You surely deserve it. All those hours of hard work and perseverance has paid off. You hear all the congratulations from your colleagues and your boss at work also.

Depending on your employer, you will surely start getting more responsibilities and you will earn the respect of your colleagues. **As you, start applying your knowledge you will demonstrate that you are capable of handling more responsibilities.**

Once you have completed CCNA, you should celebrate for a day or two. After that you have to start thinking about your next move. What is next? This will depend on a number of factors like what is your interest, what direction the company wants you to go or what are the demands in the market now a days. For example, if you are fascinated with security you may want to look at physical security, firewalls, ethical hacking, penetration testing and pursue other Cisco specialization certifications or non-vendor specific certifications such as CISSP, CEH and others. For those who are interested in a demanding and yet popular program, Voice has its own certification which has CCNA as a prerequisite. There are other similar and continuously changing certification tracks such as Data-Center, Service Provider, Wireless and others which require the fundamental of networking namely CCNA. Visit Cisco's website for the latest programs.

What We Did

I [(Vivek)] was overwhelmed with happiness when I achieved my CCNA. The company promised they would pay for my exam fees if I pass the test and I did. So I got some monetary benefits. The other thing I did was to see what to do next. By achieving CCNA certification I had proved to myself that I could do well in the field of networking. Passing CCNA was hard but it was also fun for me. In those days CCNP (R&S) was the only option to move forward and that is what I did. I started working towards my CCNP and took the CCNP Routing exam next. I told my boss and he helped me get books and study material. Later on I also got one week training on switching from the company side at the local Cisco Training Partner.

CHAPTER 10: EXPECT THIS IN YOUR EXAM

How to answer multiple choice and simulation questions

The CCNA exam is an excellent test. I say that because it tests your understanding of concepts of networking in multiple ways. There are the regular multiple choice questions and the configuration simulation questions. For multiple choice questions, you can pick one or more answers, but cannot mark any question or go back to it to make any changes.

If you see a radio button this means only one answer can be picked. On the other hand if you see a box this means two or more choices are to be made. At times it may help to read the last sentence first to know what information is relevant in case you get a lengthy question. If you are stuck with a question, look at the answers, some of the options may be incorrect and obviously wrong. This will help you narrow down the choices for the correct answer.

If you search for "Cisco Certification Exam Tutorial" in any major search engine, you may find the following link **http://www.cisco.com/web/learning/le3/learning_certification_exam_t utorial.html** (Please note that this hyperlink may change). This webpage informs you about the format of exam questions such as single answer, multiple answers, drag and drop, fill in the blanks, simulation and others. It can also provide a link to an accompanying video that shows the look and feel of the exams on the same page.

There are simulation questions that run a lighter version of IOS with limited options; therefore, it is important to get hands-on experience with IOS command structure. The hands-on would ultimately help you not to just pass the exam, but to also help you with configuration and troubleshooting in a lab or production network. Because Cisco wants you to learn to use their products thoroughly it is a possibility that the hands on labs carry more weight in your final CCNA exam score.

There might be some other variations of simulation in the exam which tests your capability of troubleshooting a network or understanding of different types of network devices.

On the day of the exam at the testing center, you need to be focused and relaxed. You will be under pressure and if you cannot maintain control normal issues that you know how to handle will become enormous.

Make sure you get a good night sleep, regardless of being ready or not, because without proper sleep you cannot do well. We highly recommend that you don't stay awake the whole night before the exam and try to cram in all the information.

CCNA exams are available in a few different languages. Select the language that you are strongest in, and most importantly, know the terminology and acronyms.

Once you pass the exam, you really need to ask yourself the following questions:

- Do I know which command and its options to use for a given situation?

- Do I know how to troubleshoot a network issue? (See our e-book "Your CCNA Success Strategy Learning by Immersing" which you can get for free. See page 190 for details.)

- Do I know where to start my troubleshooting process and how to methodically breakdown a problem and find the root cause?

The entire structure and fundamentals of these questions are covered in CCNA. Therefore it is important not to just pass the exam, but to have a good understanding of the technology also.

What Would We Do

We would prepare using the timeline (Chapter 37: Your flight plan) and stay close to it so that the day before the exam we are just reviewing and not learning anything new. The night before the exam, we would have a good night of sleep and be at the exam center on time. Once inside, we would use the time for the survey to write down all the information that we need to refer on the dry erase board using the marker provided. Once that is done, we would quickly complete the survey and close our eyes to take a deep breath so that we would be relaxed by the time the exam started. We would keep track of the time and the number of questions that we have answered. I [(Vivek)] have the habit of being in a hurry and just answering the question after reading it three fourths of the way. Please do not do that. **Don't just read the question, *understand it.*** Read the question in its entirety and then find the most appropriate answer. If all answers seem to be very similar, select the most specific answer.

This took a great amount of learning and practice. I ^(Vivek) was not skillful even after my third or fourth exam. By talking to friends who were successful I came to know about the different aspects that can trick you and have practiced that ever since.

CHAPTER 11: BUILDING YOUR FLIGHT CREW

Engaging Everyone in Your Inner Circle

Before you take the plunge and pursue your CCNA, you should make absolutely certain that everyone in your life supports your decision, especially your significant other, your children, your closest friends and family members. The CCNA exam requires total commitment, and without everyone's cooperation, it can be downright impossible to achieve. If you don't have their total support, perhaps you should consider delaying certification until circumstances are more amenable.

In this way, **you should consider certification a communal goal, rather than just a personal one.**

If you are going to work a full-time job, and still want to study for four hours a night on weekdays, and six or eight hours on the weekends, then you are going to need everyone in your household to be committed to your cause 100%, and be 100% supportive.

Everyone in your life has to make just as many sacrifices as you have to. Together, you are all going to have to weigh these considerations before making a final decision. Remember, it isn't just about the time you won't be able to devote to your friends and family. There is a great physical and mental toll, as well as a financial one.

There will be times when you need to rely on your close friends and family for emotional support, especially when you are feeling down or discouraged because you are not progressing as quickly as you would have thought. They must be your strength, and help you move forward.

Nothing in this chapter is meant to deter you from pursuing your CCNA certification. Rather, we just want you to be aware of everything you are going to encounter in the process. There are many benefits besides financial ones for your family on completion of this certification. For instance, think about the positive example you will be setting for them, as well as for yourself. You will definitely learn and acquire a new sense of perseverance. Using the newly acquired confidence and ability to study you will be able to get more certifications and further your career.

And if **you make it a group goal,** instead of a personal one, **success will be something that everyone will be proud of**.

What Would We Do

You must take into account that it will be your spouse/partner who will take up all the slack while you're off studying, and that although they are not actually taking the exam themselves, the entire process will be just as stressful for them.

Within months of starting our first certifications, we both understood very early on the importance of getting everybody onboard. To compensate, we sat down with our families and told them of our plans and what to expect. We definitely did not want to be away from home for hours, only to return to great tension, and serious arguments. By having this open and honest discussion with our entire family, and laying out our plans and expectations, everyone understood that they all had an important role to play in our success.

I ^(Dean) particularly remember a few instances when my daughter, (three years old at the time) would offer me juice or water in her most precious favorite cup when I would come back from a study session. I had truly made my study a family goal.

The sacrifices that you make during this period will pay off when you pass the exam and find yourself with plenty of time to catch up. You will have your certification, and you and your close friends and family will have the satisfaction of having achieved it as a unit.

Both of us have also set a great example for our kids. They learned that they have to concentrate and work hard for long periods of time in order to succeed.

CHAPTER 12: HOW TO HANDLE TURBULENCE

How to Deal With Road Blocks and Setbacks

One of the biggest challenges to getting your CCNA is finding a way to mitigate all the external forces that seek to blow you off course. You may experience a family emergency or an unexpected increase in your workload at the office; maybe even unforeseen financial difficulties. These are just a few of the issues that could be waiting in the wings to trip you up as you continue on your journey towards the coveted CCNA certification. Remember, studying for this certification can take a minimum of four to eight months. That's a lot of time for problems to occur.

To ensure that you stay on track (or as close to track as you can when circumstances suddenly change), and **complete your CCNA certification in a planned predictable time** we've created different timelines in Chapter 37 for the two different tracks of CCNA for you. These timelines will not only give you a good estimate of how long a CCNA certification takes, but can also help you make sure that the time you spend studying is used most effectively and efficiently. We broke down each timeline into multiple milestones with specific time to cover a particular part of the CCNA blue print.

A timeline is basically a series of steps, and the estimated time it should take for you to complete them. If you don't stick to a timeline then you will get behind schedule and it will be very difficult to catch up. For instance, most engineers start by reading the recommended books and learning the technologies related to their CCNA exam. Suppose you decide to read a book in 60 days and then start doing the labs. If you procrastinate, that deadline will approach rapidly, and the pressure will begin to mount. If you don't finish that book on time, chances are that you won't be able to start doing your labs on time either and so on. Soon, it is day 90 when you should be doing more complex labs and you have not even finished that first book. The pressure now is almost unbearable. Any more delays and you may give up.

You must not let all of these pressures build up. The more anxious you feel, the less likely you will be able to continue. Simply adjust your timeline for the current task, but keep your CCNA exam date in place. Each of the timelines in Chapter 37 has some flexibility built in. This flexibility gives you about 4 to 7 days of extra time (slack time) to take care of unknown factors and still be on schedule. If you are making too many adjustments, however, you must re-evaluate your approach. Try to figure out what is preventing you from adhering to the timeline. Perhaps you need to adjust your priorities, or change to a different timeline or just quit procrastinating.

Regardless of how much you plan and prepare, experiencing hiccups and setbacks is inevitable. Therefore, **it is important that you give priority to what really matters** and give yourself a little slack time. Please refer to the various timelines regarding the amount of slack time you can afford. This is the amount of time that you can give to other priorities without throwing your timeline off (for a short duration only).

However, **you must not rely on that slack time** and use it as an excuse to procrastinate. It is there only for emergencies, or those few issues that take precedence over your CCNA. If it can wait or can be delegated, you should do so.

If you really want to achieve one of the challenging technical certifications, **you've got to give it 100%, period**. Movie nights, hanging out with your friends, or watching football should come second. If they are not, you should really reconsider pursuing your CCNA. Remember, you can always catch up with your friends and football scores, and anything else you might have missed after you have achieved your goal of getting the CCNA certified status.

One obstacle that might affect your focus is your chain of command at work, especially if at times they may less than supportive. Communicate with them on a regular basis and let them know of your progress in your job and your CCNA.

What Would We Do

If we were to start studying for CCNA today, we would first evaluate where our knowledge lies and what is the best way for us to learn. Once that is done we would choose a timeline that gives us enough time. If the timeline in the book did not suit us, we would modify it to suit our needs. However one thing is for sure, that once we finalized the time line, we would make sure to stick to it. When we would find ourselves falling behind we would ask why, and remedy the situation. Barring any great unfortunate circumstances, **we would make sure that we are on schedule or ahead of schedule**. Every time I ^(Vivek) would procrastinate, I would give myself a difficult task or lesson to achieve in a short time to make sure I do not do that again. We would also make sure that we finish ahead of schedule, thus giving us more confidence and a sense of achievement.

CHAPTER 13: REWARD FOR YOUR SUCCESSFUL FLIGHT

Set a Clear prize for Success

Since you are about to embark on the CCNA certification, you should establish some kind of material reward to help motivate you. Some examples could be:

1. A family trip

2. Taking a cruise

3. Getting that latest mobile phone or tablet computer.

4. Getting yourself that piece of jewelry or watch that you have been looking at.

You may be wondering, why? After all, isn't the satisfaction you will feel upon passing the exam motivation enough? The answer is no. You see, the subconscious mind responds best to real, physical rewards—things that can be touched or felt. Every time you look at your new watch, see the cruise liner picture, or look at the family photos on the beach, you will be reminded of your great accomplishment.

Whatever your reward, try to get a picture of yourself with it. Select a mobile phone or tablet and have the sales person take a picture of you with it. Then inform him or her that you'll be back for it in about six months. The same goes for that watch. Go try it on, see how heavy it feels on your wrist. Get someone to take a picture. Of course, personal pictures aren't always possible, such as you on a cruise ship. In those cases, simply download a photo from the internet.

You should display these pictures prominently in your place of study, or anywhere else where you will see them regularly. Tape them to the wall above your computer, the fridge or the dashboard of your car. Carry one in your wallet. This will help give you a real, concrete goal.

What you are doing here is hanging a carrot in front of yourself. **Working for a real, tangible reward is often more effective than working toward some intangible certificate**. Once you've selected your prize that you can see, feel, dream of, or taste, your subconscious mind will automatically begin working toward it. What's more, when you finally reach your goal and get your reward, you will feel an even greater sense of accomplishment, the one that will give you the confidence to go after your next great objective.

What We Did

I [(Vivek)] did not develop this technique till I started studying for my first CCIE Lab exam. For my CCNA I was just studying hard from the book and would work late in the office after hours to get hands on experience on Cisco hardware. (There were no IOS simulators at that time). I spent long hours working on basic configurations because I did not have a mentor. All this was taking a toll on my family life. When my wife asked me to why I was working so hard, I told her about all the advantages and doors that would open for me. I also mentioned that my boss had told me that he would pay my exam fees if I passed the test. At that moment, it occurred to me that I could take my wife out to a very nice luxurious restaurant for a great memorable dinner with that money and that is what I eventually did.

Since then, I have used this technique to get myself motivated to pass many other certifications. Each certification got me something tangible for myself or something that would create a memory for a lifetime for me and my family.

CHAPTER 14: THE FIRST KEY TO SUCCESS

Set Your Goals and Write Them Down

In our experience, many network engineers who want to be a CCNA are all too often overwhelmed by many of the factors we've already warned you about. We don't want you to be overwhelmed, so here is what you should do.

You are obviously going to set your goal of getting your CCNA certification, but we want you to be more specific. We even want you to select a specific date. For instance, "I am going to get my CCNA certified status by November 14th, 2015." The more specific you are, the better it is.

As soon as you set this date, we want you to write it down. Post your goal date (like the pictures of your tangible reward) where it will be easily visible to you. Make multiple copies if you have to, set it as the screensaver or background image on your computer.

You should then share your intentions with as many of your family, friends, and colleagues. What you are doing here is making your goals concrete, creating a public commitment, and holding yourself accountable.

The effectiveness of this strategy was recently established by a Dominican University study.

You may have heard the story of a Harvard (or Yale) study that took place in the late 50s, 60s, or even 70s, in which the 3% of students who actually wrote down their goals were shown, 20 years later, to earn as much as ten times more than those who did not. This was discovered by Dominican University, and others, to be an urban legend, so they decided to test the hypothesis themselves. They took a group of 267 participants and broke them into five groups. Each of these groups was asked to adhere to a different level of commitment. The first group was asked to merely think about their goals. The second group was asked to think about their goal and write it down. The third group was asked to think about their goal, write it down, and establish action steps. The fourth group was asked to think about their goal, write it down, formulate action steps, and share their plan with a friend. The fifth group was asked to think about their goal, write it down, formulate action steps, share their plan with a friend, and then keep that friend updated on their progress as they pursued their goal.

In the end, the **groups who simply put their goals on paper were significantly more likely to achieve their goals than those who did not,** while those in group five were even more likely to succeed than any of the others.

If you'd like to read the study for yourself, you can see a summary here:

http://www.dominican.edu/dominicannews/study-backs-up-strategies-for-achieving-goals

It's human nature to procrastinate, to try to find the easy way out. We tend to postpone the most difficult tasks until an undetermined date in the future. To make matters worse, we live in an age in which everyone expects instant results. Nobody wants to wait for anything, especially not for months. Cisco certification tracks are a long-term commitment, and it's not going to get any easier as time passes. In fact, if anything CCNA is going to get harder as new technologies are introduced. If you don't finish now, when will you?

The most important thing you can do is try to pass the exam before Cisco makes any major revisions to the test. Your training provider should be able to inform you of any expected changes. Make sure you are prepared.

CHAPTER 15: THE SECOND KEY TO SUCCESS

Visualize; Behave As If you've Already Achieved It

We are big believers in the power of visualization. We visualized this book even before we began writing it. We knew exactly how it would look, its size, thickness, how many chapters it would have, and how heavy it would feel in our hands. We kept this visualization going even when we had our first draft ready. The first draft looked very similar to the final book. Visualization is a very powerful and effective tool. The more detailed and targeted your visuals are, the more effective they become.

For example, think of your favorite food, a bowl of hot tomato soup, a juicy fish fillet, a delicious muffin or a red velvet cake. As you read this just close your eyes for a second and visualize them. Did you start salivating? I know I am. I have this great urge to eat something sweet right now.

Visualizing stimulates the same parts of your brain that would have been affected by seeing, smelling, and tasting the real thing. If the visuals are appealing enough, your brain will subconsciously start working toward making this into a reality. You will soon start seeing positive signs, things rolling almost magically into place. This is called synchronicity, which can be defined as a "meaningful coincidence."

Your eyes gather all of the information from your surroundings, but the brain, being a super-efficient organ, doesn't process all of it. It filters out the irrelevant and only processes the important stuff. For example, let's say you were planning to buy a particular model car. Since this information is simmering somewhere in your subconscious, you will suddenly start seeing those cars everywhere. Now, of course, they'd been there all along, you just weren't aware of them. You may also start seeing great deals, or unexpected bargains and opportunities that you would have easily overlooked before.

By visualizing that car, you've created a clear goal for yourself. Your mind wants to fulfill that goal, to satisfy that desire.

The same is true of your CCNA. **Once you get your mind going towards a goal, through visualization, it starts looking for ways to achieve it**. It subconsciously starts steering you toward applicable articles in magazines, and websites, and towards knowledgeable people. You may even find yourself regularly, almost inexplicably, overhearing conversations involving the words "CCNA" or "CCNP" or "Cisco Certification."

If it helps, you can think of this process in terms of a network. What your brain is doing is opening a port that allows only interesting information in; the rest is simply excluded, in the same way that a firewall might allow only relevant traffic to pass through and blocks everything else.

At one time or another, we have all been passed over for a promotion because we did not have the right qualifications. Instead of blaming your boss, the long working hours, the family circumstances, your luck, yourself, or being envious of your colleagues, you should use this to **fuel the fire of**

intention, and propel yourself toward the position of your desire.

What We Did

We all have seen action replays in our favorite games of basketball, baseball, soccer or cricket. Visualization is performing the action in your mind; the action replay happens when you are actually doing it.

This book that you are holding in your hands is the result of that action replay.

An artist visualizes that painting in his/her mind and when he starts painting, it is all an action replay of his visualization.

At the time when we did our CCNA we did not know about the power of visualization. Somewhere along the line of doing certifications, we started to visualize and it has helped us ever since.

CHAPTER 16: THE THIRD KEY TO SUCCESS

All or Nothing

There's an interesting dichotomy between what we humans expect of other people (and things in life) and what we'll accept from ourselves. For instance, we expect our food to be cooked to our taste 100% of the time. We also expect our electricity and our phone service to run uninterrupted 100% of the time. We expect the doctor to be able to cure our ailment or the police to catch a perpetrator 100% of the time. However, when it comes to our own activities, we're often content to lower our expectations. We might be happy with 99%, or 95%, sometimes even 75%. After all, 75% of perfect is a lot better than nothing at all, right?

But just imagine what would happen if pilots and doctors were held to the same standards. Would you be willing to trust your life to a pilot who was only careful 75% of the time? Would you submit to surgery at the hands of a doctor who was only willing to put in a half-hearted effort, so that he could get in time to watch the game?

Of course you wouldn't. But all too often, we find ourselves procrastinating, then doing an inadequate job, just to complete it as quickly as possible so that we can move on to something more interesting or engaging. In these instances, being thorough or meticulous gets thrown overboard.

Certification requires total commitment and painstaking attention to

detail, not just 75% of the time, nor even 99% of the time, but a full 100% of the time.

That's not to say that there aren't activities in life that you can't get away with giving less than 100 % of your effort.

A very successful boxing coach used to demand that his boxers make an effort to run (what is called "roadwork" in boxing) every day, without question. He explained to his boxers that he was preparing them for the unexpected, that you never knew if something was going to come up tomorrow that would prevent you from achieving your goal. And while you may not lose the endurance that roadwork provided by missing one day, you certainly would if you missed anymore.

If your effort is 95% or 99%, then you have some wiggle room to postpone or have the chance of something else taking priority. We're not saying that you should stop everything else. After all, the lawn will still need to be mowed, and the dishes will still need to be done. What we are saying is that if you've allocated four hours every evening for study, you shouldn't let anything interfere with that. **Giving 100% to your CCNA certification means that it has priority**. If you have to sacrifice or postpone something, it should be the things that are lower priority. After all, that grass isn't going to stop growing, and it's not going anywhere, is it? You can easily delegate it to someone; defer doing that until a later date or during a study break. Nothing comes between you and your studies during the time you specifically allocated for CCNA Certification. The earlier you start following and learning this, the better it will be for you.

What Would We Do

When we were preparing for our CCNA we used to hear this from many other engineers: "I have been studying slowly but never get the time, so I am going to book my CCNA exam date and then I will be able to study".

I am sure you have heard the same many times too. You hear this not only for certification but for filing your taxes, getting that crack in your car windshield repaired, and going to the post office to pick up your parcel. This is a strategy that does work and will eventually make you to get your work done after procrastinating. As soon as the last date of filing your taxes approaches or the crack in the windshield becomes too big or the post office calls that they will send the parcel back, you spring into action and get the work done.

Unfortunately, **this does not work for CCNA certification**. You cannot start studying three days or a week before the CCNA exam and pass. It requires much more preparation and dedication so do not fall into this trap.

We would never fall into this trap and would make our own timeline using the guidance in Chap 37 and prepare for our CCNA exam.

CHAPTER 17: USING THE KEYS

The Three-Key Combination

Over the course of the last few chapters, we have given you **the three keys to success**. Now, we are going to show you how to put them all together in a way that will help you pass the CCNA exam and have the CCNA certified status.

To illustrate this, I [(Vivek)] am going to tell you a little story. When I was a child, I was fascinated by bank safety deposit boxes and how they operated. I especially liked how they were always located inside a huge vault. Stepping into it was like entering a large safe. The walls were made of eight to ten inches of solid steel and the bolts were these huge shiny cylinders that slid into their recesses, which made the room virtually impenetrable without the proper key or combination. Once inside, it seemed even more clandestine and mysterious. The banker came in with his key and you had your key, and you needed both of them, turned almost in tandem, to open the safety deposit box.

To access your safety deposit box **there were three keys that were essential**.

1. The key or the combination to the vault.

2. Your key to the safety deposit box.

3. Bankers key to the safety deposit box.

With these three keys being used together your access to the contents of the safety deposit box happened with little effort. But even if **one of the keys was missing, there is no way you could access** the contents.

The previous three chapters are like your keys to the safety deposit box that has your CCNA certified status. Success becomes a lot easier and assured if you use these keys.

1. Setting your goal.

2. Visualizing your goal.

3. Giving it your 100%.

If you don't **use all these keys together and in tandem** the safety deposit box will not open, which means you will not be CCNA certified.

CHAPTER 18: PRE-FLIGHT CHECK

So you decided to do your CCNA, now what?

You should be proud of yourself for starting this endeavor. I say this because you have decided to boldly step into the world of networking which you do not know much about. You know that you will have to learn new technologies and grasp new concepts, which is never easy. The one thing you must remember, though, that the ultimate goal is not just to pass an exam, it is to have the CCNA certified status that shows the world that you have arrived in the field of networking. This may seem counter-intuitive at first since you must pass an exam before you can get your CCNA Certified status, but it's all about training your brain. You see, when you set CCNA certified status as your goal, the exam becomes just one more step in the process. In this way, not passing the exam becomes merely a minor setback—one bump in the road rather than a roadblock. Your brain seeks to fulfill your goals, and if the goal is to pass the exam and you don't, your mind interprets this as a failure. However, if the goal is to get your CCNA certified status, your mind will work on it until you get it.

You can get a good idea of what you need to read and what books to use as a reference on Cisco's website, CCNA blueprint. We would also suggest that you spend some time researching CCNA training providers. Contact them directly and ask if they offer any special promotions. Who knows, you may get a good discount. When looking for the right training provider, keep in mind they should have the most up to date program relating to Cisco's latest exam. For instance, they should be able to guide you on how to handle the simulation section of the exam, or make you aware of any upcoming changes in the CCNA exam. You should also talk to as many other engineers as possible. Find out what strategies worked best for them, and what potential pitfalls might await you.

Note: There are an overwhelming number of free resources available on the internet for CCNA. So you might ask me, why not use those? Yes you can use those but you will have to spend a very long time sorting through what is correct and what is not. You also don't know if the information is up to date or how accurate it is. If you have a close friend or a mentor whom you can believe in, and they just passed CCNA, then follow their advice about free resources. I am not saying that it is wrong to use free resources, but when you start studying for the CCNA you are new to the subject and if you learn it in an organized fashion from a training provider you will be able to reach your goal much faster. One may argue about the money you spend on training and we would counter the argument with the fact that the number of months you saved in studying will pay you back much more, because you will be getting a better paying job earlier.

Once you've decided on a CCNA training provider and a program, you should stick with it. Each CCNA training provider offers a variety of programs to suit different learning styles. **Jumping from one to the other**

could disrupt the flow and cause confusion. The most important thing to understand at this point is that **there are no shortcuts**. In the end, you must learn the content and complete the practice labs. Think of it this way: in order to gain muscle, you've got to lift weights. No one can do that for you. However, a good trainer can help you gain muscle faster--and more effectively--by focusing your exercise routine. Imagine your CCNA training provider as the trainer in the CCNA Olympics gym and your goal is to get the gold medal– your own CCNA certified status. Your courseware should tell you in great detail about all the technical aspects, but your training provider will help you maximize the results.

We feel that within two weeks of signing up with the training provider of your choice, you should have your study routine, hardware, and software for the lab ready. If you are using router simulator, such as DYNAMIPS/GNS3, you should also have a powerful computer. Now is the time to choose a timeline. Look at the different timelines at the end of this book for guidance (Chapter 37). Regardless of which timeline you choose, set the first target date to check your progress at about six weeks. Based on the progress made in these six weeks, you should decide if you want to follow the study time line you have already chosen. I say this because this is a good time to customize your study timeline. Make all the adjustments now. Give yourself enough time. We do not recommend changing your study schedule after this point. (See Chapter 21 "Practice hard and play even harder") Check the CCNA exam availability and adjust your schedule accordingly. Remember that the exam dates during certain times of the year (especially during and after holidays and weekends) are harder to get.

What Would We Do

Let's use a practical example. Suppose you are going to Paris for vacation. You can explore Paris in three different ways

1. Get an official Guide for yourself or be a part of a guided tour. If you choose the latter, you will have seen the main city highlights without any problems in 3 to 5 days. The guided tour will take you to the right places without issues and at the best times and may have discounted tickets for many attractions.

2. You do your own research but use the L'Open Tour Paris Hop on Hop off Sightseeing Buses to explore the city on your own terms and your own will. This will take more time than the first option but will eventually take you to most of the places that a guided tour will take. Please note I say most of the places, not all.

3. The last option is you reach Paris and then ask around and may be go to the Eiffel tower as you have heard about, then ask around about what the next best place is and go on from there. You are depending on strangers whom you talk to and their choice of what is best to look at next, and how to reach there. This gives you the maximum flexibility, but will take an excruciatingly long time and you will never be sure you have visited all the good sites in the city.

Always take the first approach or a mix of the first and second approach. Why reinvent the wheel? A good training provider has trained so many students so take advantage of their experience. It is like getting in a class with a good teacher that makes the subject look easy. This also takes the least amount of time. Now of course you have to pay for this, but think of it this way, it is an investment that will pay you back in a few months as soon as you get a better job because of CCNA (see Chapter 7 "Investing in yourself").

Note: There are many CCNA engineers in the market today who have a paper certification. By that I mean that they somehow read the book or exam dumps but do not understand the technologies. As a result, they go for interviews and fail miserably. Those are the ones who end up saying that CCNA is useless. To me, it looks like they took the third approach to explore Paris and are now saying, "What is the big deal about Paris? It is like any other city."

Note: Although most of the training providers are good but there are some unscrupulous ones that guarantee 100% success after a one week course. We would be very wary of such training providers.

CHAPTER 19: THE AIR TRAFFIC CONTROLLER

The importance of mentors

A mentor is defined as "a wise and trusted counselor, an influential supporter, someone who is more experienced, who advises and guides a less experienced person." You might not know that many organizations have mentorship programs. If yours does not, you can approach any of the senior staff and they will probably be flattered to be a mentor. Other ways to find a good mentor are CCNA Groups, online forums and online communities like Google groups and LinkedIn. YouTube has many great videos from experts also.

The mentors would be able to explain the technologies and answer your questions in a manner that is understandable to you and allows them to polish their skills. Remember teaching is the best form of learning.

Keep in mind a couple of things:

- Be considerate with their time. Ask them specific questions. They are not there to spoon feed you.

- Have more than one mentor so you can leverage their strengths and balance the time.

Mentorship should have a start and end date; you do not want to be mentored for years. Instead you may want to pick your mentor for duration of few months during which you may be able to make requests for assistance. **This relationship should be such that both parties will be**

benefiting from each other.

Please keep in mind that once you pass the exam, you may want to become a mentor to another engineer. This way you give back to the networking community and also have a chance to learn more about the technology as teaching is learning.

Now you will ask, "How do I choose a mentor?" Here are the criteria's for that.

1. Your mentor should have the specific knowledge that you seek (i.e. should have a CCNA or higher certification).

2. Your mentor should have recent knowledge (CCNA has newer topics like IPv6.)

3. Knowing and being able to teach are two different things. Your mentor should be able to teach. I have seen great engineers who confuse you more when they explain things to you. This does not mean that they are bad teachers, it is just that their teaching style is not compatible with your learning style or they are not able to simplify the technology enough to make you understand.

4. Your mentor should not only have spare time but un-interrupted time for you so that you can ask questions and he/she can answer you to your satisfaction. You can't have your mentor on a conference call and trying to answer your questions at the same time.

5. Your mentor's free time should be preferably in sync with your

free time. If you work the morning shift and your mentor works the evening shift, you will hardly have any time to talk to him.

6. Your mentor should be approachable at different hours. I say this because if you are stuck in your lab at 8 PM you should be able to call and get help.

7. Your mentor should be such that you are be able to ask them even the smallest or most fundamental questions without hesitation. What I mean here is that if your mentor is your supervisor, you may hesitate to ask him all the questions because of the fear of being judged as someone who does not even know something basic.

8. A mentor should usually feel happiness in helping and should be very cooperative. But on the other hand, the mentor should also know how to push you to work hard and should not spoon feed you or make you dependent on him.

9. You will be exposing your weaknesses to your mentor and therefore the mentor you choose should be someone that you trust and feel comfortable with, you don't want them to be making fun of you or talking about you with others and you also don't want to your mentor to belittle you or your questions.

10. It is preferred that you should be able to meet face to face with your mentor. However in this technological age you can virtually connect with a mentor who may be anywhere.

What Would We Do

We would choose a mentor with great care using the criteria above and also make sure that we try and ask intelligent questions. If you ask the question the right way, you can get a very helpful answer. For example, instead of asking how to configure OSPF I would ask how to configure OSPF when one side is a Point to Point link and the other side is a Point to Multipoint link?

We would not hesitate to connect with a mentor online. If the mentor is really good then we will not mind him/her being in another country or time zone. We would even pay for their services. We can always connect with them using instant messaging, voice messaging and other online resources. Having a mentor in another country or time zone may have some constraints but having a good mentor will make us reach our CCNA certified status much faster and that is as good as gold.

CHAPTER 20: PILOT AND CO-PILOT

Choose your partner wisely

Learning your CCNA topics and technologies involves a lot of self-studying where you need to be on your own. A partner is not necessary, but highly recommended because a partner could be very helpful.

You can ask your partner:

1. Why do you think this works?

2. Why do you think this does not work?

3. Can we do this in a different way?

There are people who prefer to work independently, but we have noticed that the majority of successful candidates had study partners. After all, you don't know the answer to everything and having someone else to ask questions is truly invaluable. Having a study partner also makes you a better learner through the ability to discuss any questions that either one of you may have. It is a proven fact that when accomplishing a challenging task, working with a partner benefits both partners, providing them with an ability to see something from another person's point of view and approach the problem differently. You can also cut down on preparation time by assigning each partner to prepare certain topics and then teaching each other. As we said earlier, we learn what we teach. Selecting a study partner depends on numerous factors, including, but not limited to personality, study habits, location and technical background.

You want to choose a partner to compliment your strengths and assist in your weaknesses.

In our experience, having one or a maximum of two partners is sufficient. Having more minds looking at a problem can get it resolved faster. It also helps you when you have more questions about a specific technology. Usually, you will be strong in certain technologies while your partner may be strong in others. This complements your study and a team effort will speed up your work.

It would be a good idea to look for these qualities in your study partner.

1. They should be of similar experience and intelligence levels. We are not saying to get an IQ test, but if you are answering all the questions and not getting your questions answered it is not going to last long.

2. Your knowledge of technologies should complement each other.

3. Personalities and temperaments should be taken into account.

4. Your partner should bring a positive attitude and be part of the solution and not the problem. You want to work with someone who sees the glass half full and not half empty.

5. It is important to choose a study partner who can make a commitment to devote their time until the completion of the certification. Dropping a partner midway disrupts the flow and equilibrium that you have established and may disturb your

progress and time of completion.

6. Your partner should be approachable at any hour, in the same time zone and it is preferred that they live nearby so that you are able to study together face to face.

7. Your partner should have the same time schedule at least on the weekends when you would be studying together.

8. You and your partner should be able to complete the tasks that you have assigned to yourselves for that week.

9. Your partner will be one that can push you to finish one more task in the lab or work on the next attempt and help you answer your questions. **Partners are there to be supportive, to ensure that you don't quit and to keep you on track.** You also need to make sure that you keep this in mind; if you choose a study partner who has already scheduled his CCNA exam two weeks from now and you haven't started any practice labs, that partnership will not be beneficial.

We emphasize again that these are not rules but just guidelines to follow. Every engineer has his own unique situation and expectations and these should be modified or used as a guide according to that.

CHAPTER 21: PRACTICE HARD AND PLAY EVEN HARDER

Study aggressively with your goal in sight

In our personal opinion, the best way to approach CCNA certification is to have a moderately aggressive plan. Work hard to make sure that you are executing your plan. If you drag your goal, after a few weeks, you will realize that it is harder to get back on track and soon it feels like your goal is too large and you begin to procrastinate and give up.

You have access to an overwhelming amount of resources; the CCNA blue print is large. Buying every CCNA book, flash card, VoD and other resources is one strategy but that may not be the best. Just jumping in and start doing labs and studying chapters selectively is not a good strategy either.

We have compiled different strategic study timelines for **engineers with different skills sets**; these study timelines are there to assist you in navigating the best appropriate path for you. We have taken the content from the CCNA blue print and broken it down into daily and weekly events which would cover a single exam track for composite exam and dual exam track for ICND1 and ICND2. **Keep in mind that, these timelines are a framework and may not necessarily be a perfect fit for you and your study partner.** These give you a starting point on which you can adjust and build your own timeline (See Chapter 37 "Your flight plan"). For example, if you are strong in routing then you can spend extra time on other topics or just shorten your time line for preparation. On the other hand if you feel you need more time, feel free to extend your time line to suit yourself. However, do not keep changing it midway.

Remember that if you put 100% into this endeavor you will have your CCNA certified status within a few months and will not have to go through this for three years when your re-certification time comes up. Recertification will be less intense and since you already know all of these technologies it's just a matter of learning the differences. We are sure that by the time of renewal you would be working on another higher level certification that will not only renew your CCNA but also make you eligible for that next higher certification. With 100% commitment, you will get the results; otherwise, success would be nearly impossible; do something, don't let excuses get in your way.

What Would We Do

When studying for any certification we make sure that when it comes to the exploratory phase wherein we are learning newer technologies or new things we study together so that we can divide our learning and teach other. For the labs, we would want to do those individually and would disturb each other only when one of us has been stuck for more than 30 minutes and has exhausted all options.

We made sure that we were in sync when doing labs (doing the same labs on the weekends) so that we could ask for each other's help if needed.

There were times when one of us got stuck at the same point as the other. Instead of telling the answer we would hint towards a document or a group of commands. This helped in solving our problems and learning how to troubleshoot. Giving away the answer would be the last resort.

We would even make complex networks and then put in configurations issues and ask each other to troubleshoot that network. This was not only fun but a fantastic way of learning to troubleshoot.

CHAPTER 22: SCHEDULE A FLIGHT PLAN AND STICK TO IT

Schedule your study hours

If you have already planned your study schedule, you have to stick to it. You may find it hard to get back on track if you miss a day or two. Don't let it slide; get back on track and start working the schedule until it becomes a habit. Regardless of what anyone does, you need to find your own suitable timeline that works best for you, your family, your mentor and finally, your study partner.

Make sure to start your routine every weekday on time as if you are going to work—for now this will be your second job.

As a part of our schedule, we made sure to have a primary and backup place to study. In the U.S., libraries are a great place to study. They even have study rooms where you can discuss and work on your lab. Other places such as coffee shops, your home office, and local university campuses should be considered.

Each of our study timelines (see Chapter 37 "Suggested Timelines for CCNA Preparation") have some slack time which acts as a buffer for the hours that you may miss due to extremely urgent situations that may emerge during the time you are studying for your CCNA.

Another cautionary note: Once you make a customized timeline that suits you the best, try it out for 4 to 6 weeks. Make a one-time adjustment if you need to but do not make any changes after that.

What We Did

We always try to be ahead of the schedule so that we can handle a few days of delays without feeling overwhelmed and tense about our goal. It is rare that we do not finish on time. We made sure that if we ever had to miss a daily morning study session because of work, we would make up the hours missed even if we were ahead of schedule. Because of this attitude we are never in a panic situation a few days before any exam that we take.

CHAPTER 23: STICK TO YOUR ETA

Time is a resource. How to use it, how to find it

One of the most important resources that you have to manage is your time, and you need to make a plan and stick to it. After having your family on board, (see Chapter 11 "Building your flight crew"), you may want to talk to your boss about this endeavor. Try to get your boss to be your advocate as this allows you more time for preparation and flexible working hours during these months of preparation.

Once your family and your boss are on board, it is a matter of planning, sheer grit and determination to use this time and these resources to achieve the goal.

As mentioned earlier, you may have to re-prioritize your goals, as well as your time that you would have spent for other activities, such as watching TV. One of the things that we always ask anyone who is going to pursue certifications, is how many hours do you spend watching TV? Most of them don't even realize that they are spending more time in front of a box than they realize. Point being, you need to manage your time and always focus on your efforts. Always think, **"How does this activity help with my CCNA certification?"** If it is not directly related to CCNA, you may want to cut or reconsider the amount of time put into it.

We all have our routines and it seems impossible to find and devote so much time to studying. Time is available, but are you using it to your advantage? How do you get thirty or forty hours in one week when you already have a family, full time job or are taking care of others?

From our experience and interviews with successful certified engineers, we found that you have to find the best time that you feel ready, alert and have minimal distractions. Feed the CCNA animal in you and leverage your time accordingly. For example, manage your commute to avoid the rush hour and instead use that time to practice small labs or study a Video-on-Demand (VoD).

You may start doing the prep work for your studies in the morning, and then finish your preparations during lunchtime so that you are ready to use every minute of your precious study time in the evening. Regardless, if there is a will, you will find a way. You need to create your own study schedule and make it suit your needs.

You need to use every free moment to your advantage. Therefore, we recommend that you print out information (flash cards, articles and configurations) to be available within arm's reach and review it, as soon as you find fifteen minutes or more time available. You may also want to have Audio-on-Demand (AoD) or VoD available to you on your laptop or on your smart phone so that you can watch and/or listen any time. For example, you are going to your child's game and it will be a thirty minute drive; bring along few pages about a topic that you need to ramp up on or listen to on the drive over. If you use public transportation to go to work, use that time to read, watch a VoD or just take a quick nap so that you're refreshed by the time you reach home. Doing this will enable you to use your time wisely. You may be surprised to find that you are able to grasp a new or difficult concept in that time.

You want to be just like a child with a new video game; all of his time is spent playing. He is steadfast in his ambition and concentration of the game. A child will play and focus every waking moment of the day on the game and everything else is just a distraction—this is how your passion for the CCNA certification should be.

The above approach has one caution; don't sacrifice your sleep or your health. If you want to have effective and fruitful results, then get your rest. If your body needs seven to eight hours of sleep then give it time to rejuvenate and heal itself.   The worst thing that you can do is to wake up tired, cranky, and ineffective.

What We Did

Once our routine was established, we used to wake up in the morning without an alarm and would practice our lab or start a new setup. Both of us found that morning hours were the best for dealing with challenging topics. That would be when we could focus the most and we knew we could grasp the technology that gave us a hard time the night before. There were instances when Dean or I [(Vivek)] woke up to a much better understanding of a concept that we struggled with on the previous nights. If you immerse yourself into this project, you may start having dreams about some of these topics and at times the answers will come to you then. Working in the morning had one more advantage: we could look up any questions or concerns during our workday whenever we had 15 minutes of time to spare.

We also made sure that everything was setup for our studies in the morning the night before. Which meant that all the relevant books, labs, notes, pens, papers were all there on the study table. All we had to do was to wake up and start studying without wasting any precious study time.

CHAPTER 24: BOOKS/VIDEOS/LAB RESOURCES

Use of training options

The training resources available to us today range from an intense boot camp course, live online education, Video On Demand (VoD), Audio on Demand (AoD), instructor led courses, seminars, as well as Cisco Live Sessions geared towards the various certification tracks and many others. Although you may be tempted to do a couple of the above, you need choose what works best for you.

Each one of us has a different style of learning, so you have to choose the resources that are best suited for you. You may be tempted to use them all. The only drawback is that it will take a long time to study all of them in detail and the longer it takes; the greater the chance that you may drop your CCNA study and the exam topics may even change.

Our suggestion is that you choose your own learning methodology, create a plan and choose the best training provider according to your plan. Once you do this, stick with that training. Use other options as additional supplements in achieving your goal. In other words, don't stretch yourself too thin, as this will overwhelm you. Many items such as books, AoD, VoD and lectures are great resources and should be used on an as-needed basis depending on what you like.

Instructor led and virtual classes are very popular and are one of the main training tools used by many companies to develop their employee's skills. It is important to realize that taking a two week boot camp will not make you an expert. To be effective, you have to prepare ahead of time. For those folks who just walk into this boot camp and expect to learn everything in two compact weeks and pass the exam in one shot without any prior preparation, the odds are not in your favor.

CCNA is meant to reflect today's real life network with its complexity. Therefore, without proper background and preparation, you will most likely not be able to succeed in your goal of being a CCNA. Some studies show that about 20% to 30% of the class curriculum will be retained by students, especially when the material is totally new to them. This means that you will not able to retain more than 70% of the material. We highly recommend that you read the self-study books or refer to them for the sections that you are having problems with and get hands on practice by trying to simulate the commands on a simulator or live gear, before attending any instructor led classes. Hands on practice and simulation are key-especially for those who have never worked on Cisco equipment. The more you prepare the more you can retain from the training session. This would substantially increase your chances of passing the exam.

VoD is also a very popular medium of study now-a-days. These technical videos are not something that you should be watching in the background as you are multitasking. The best way to use these videos is to study them, simulate the network that is being used in the VoD and try what is being taught through hands on practice. The majority of the CCNA protocols that you are expected to know are used in the real production network environment, so you need to know it and you need to love it!

You have to have flexibility and determination to keep studying and moving towards your goal of having a CCNA Certified Status. You need to find time regularly either in the morning or the evening to study. If for any reason you have to miss the morning study time, make sure that you make up for it the same evening or the next day. Think of it this way; if you skip one meal you can eat more the same day. However, if you don't eat for a whole day, you cannot make it up by eating twice as much the next day. Like your stomach, there is a limit to what your mind can absorb. This is the very reason we have made these learning timelines (See chapter 37 "Your flight plan") so that you can follow them and be assured that this will keep you on track and will increase your chances of becoming CCNA certified.

Instead of memorizing the practice labs, **understand the concepts behind each lab.** The confidence that you generate after completing a few labs successfully will be the catalyst for your success.

What Would We Do

When we did our CCNA, books and a one week class were the only options available for us. So we read the book cover to cover at least three times and made sure that we could not only answer the questions at the end of every chapter but we also understood the technologies. If we were doing our CCNA today, we would read the official training guide or certification book for a basic understanding and then start learning from the VoD. We would also simulate the VoD exercises on our simulator to practice and learn. Doing hands on labs would give us the familiarity with the Cisco IOS CLI. This will not only help in the CCNA exam but will also give us the confidence that we will be able to work on live routers and switches in real world situations. Lastly we would use the technique described in the next chapter to learn the most from VoD.

CHAPTER 25: VOD

How to exploit Videos on Demand

There are many learning resources available, but we prefer Video-on-Demand (VoD). Why? Because, we like the visual format and are able to learn at our own pace and go back and forth. If you choose to take the VoD option, we have some helpful advice. VoD also means that although you hear and see everything, you also need to read the book and understand the subject.

At the onset, create the same network being used in the VoD on your simulator or lab. As you are listening to the VoD, make note of the time when a particular topic starts and ends. This will let you to go back to the same point to review. This is a huge timesaver and allows you to learn new technologies effectively.

Here is a four-step process that we used to ensure that we had mastered the Video-on-Demand:

Step 1: Watch and listen to one complete video and understand the basic concepts.

Step 2: Now start the video again, and this time pause, taking detailed notes on the topics you think you may be weak in or need to review.

Step 3: Using your notes, simulate the VoD network in your lab. Hands-on experience reinforces and crystallizes the whole topic into your brain.

Step 4: Go back to Video on Demand, and this time validate, and compare the VoD with your simulation work. This way, you will be able to identify any of the mistakes that you have made.

You may still have a few questions, but those can be answered by reading a book, consulting your mentor or through training provider forums. You can also ask your partner or colleagues.

This process is tedious but works very well. At the outset, it may take longer, but will save you a lot of time later on. To get your partner involved, go to an environment where you will be able to talk, watch the videos together and show your work. Being in the same room with your study partner is much more productive than studying remotely. Expect the learning from Video-on-Demand to take some time, if you are not in the same room, at which time you can use web based sharing technologies to coordinate your work.

We have seen other engineers who have taken elaborate notes with the help of hyperlinks, PDF content and other reference points. This comprehensive and sophisticated knowledge-base is splendid if you can keep up with the milestones on your timeline.

Try using different methods and technologies in your lab by using the question mark in the commands. Use various options and see the effect on your lab network.

This will help you a lot in learning the features and will also enable you to answer those tricky questions or come up with workarounds as you make your way through the lab. Finding ways to break your network helps in building your troubleshooting skills.

What Would We Do

There was no VoD available for CCNA when I ^(Vivek) was studying for this exam. I utilized the Video on Demand approach for learning technologies fully for other certifications and while doing that I came up with this four-step process of learning that is mentioned earlier in this chapter. Simulating the VoD network seemed like an uphill task initially but once it was done I had learned a lot. This was because I had the freedom to explore different options and see what happens if I do this or I do that. There were times when I brought the network down totally but it was ok as it was my lab network and not a real live network. Hands on learning techniques are the best possible way of learning especially for technical certifications.

CHAPTER 26: THE FLIGHT SIMULATOR

Use of labs to learn a specific technology

Learn to work the labs when learning the technologies. CCNA hands-on experience on a live corporate network is not necessary to pass the exam, but hands on practical experience is a must for any network engineer. Remember that when outages occur you will not have multiple choice questions to solve the issue. You must know what each command does, what it means and how the options in each command are used. The question mark (?) is your friend, it is essential to know the IOS command structure.

In order to get the necessary hands-on you may use any IOS simulators. There are some available on Internet for free as well as accompanying videos to show and walk you through the installation and use of these simulators. Some books also have a simulator on the accompanying CD/DVD.

One method of learning IOS hierarchical structure is to run different option and use of help (?) should always be part of your lab exercises. This would help you on the exam simulation questions as well as during network troubleshooting.

Simulating a network with frame relay links and serial links will give you good practice for WAN technologies. Making a simulation with VLAN's, DHCP, trunks etc. gives you good practice on LAN technologies. You can even combine these two in your own way to make your own simulated enterprise network which will be your personal playing field.

Many books as part of their training will provide you with a lab scenario and show the commands for that scenario. You will learn what each command is used for and what important parameters you need to know from each command. Each show command is made to illustrate information, but not all of it may be relevant to your problem. Therefore, for every show command, we pick and choose the information we need. It is imperative to know what command gives you what information. For example, you should know that if you want to see which interfaces of a router are configured with an IP address, you can use the "show ip interface brief" command. If you want to see which interfaces on your switch are using what type of optical interface you can use the "show interface status" command. After your simulated network is up, run the show commands and check all the information that the book is indicating to you as significant. For example, if you run the show interface command make sure you are able to see if the interface is up or down, interface errors, interface speed and duplex etc. These show commands are used every day in the networking world and regardless of your skill level or the certification to capture information. **The same show commands that we use in CCNA are also used by CCNP and even CCIE's** in real live production networks. This simulation process would give you the sense of confidence as if you are in the real network environment, even though you are running them on your simulator.

What We Did

When we started to learn, simulation seemed difficult. However, after simulating two or three small networks, it became much easier. After that we started combining these small networks into larger networks. Soon we could easily simulate networks that were complex and had a combination of different technologies. We would then make the network work with RIP. Maybe a week later we could run the same network with EIGRP. Change serial links to point-to-point links or add a hub and spoke frame relay to our network.

Working on all these networks was a lot of fun. Well, it was fun when it worked. We would sometimes spend hours working on a network problem and found ourselves frustrated. However, those hours of reading and troubleshooting gave us the understanding that eventually made us successful engineers and eventually CCIE's.

CHAPTER 27: KEEP FIT

Healthy body for a sound mind

When you start spending long hours preparing for the CCNA exam, there are changes that will happen to your body. Weight gain is one huge factor. Don't forget you are sitting behind a computer on a daily basis, sometimes for hours at a time. Expect it and don't stress out over it.

Keep your mind sharp and your body healthy during this stressful period. One good approach to manage stress is to exercise regularly. Perhaps doing some Yoga, Tai-chi or other meditation movement will clear your mind. I [(Dean)] often practice yoga by following a series of videos and doing them any time I feel overwhelmed with work or am under any sort of stress. Others have stated that doing cardiovascular movement would increase blood flow to your brain and get your heart pumping. Whatever works for you and will not hurt or injure you.

During our studies, I [(Dean)] was getting tired, and found myself unable to focus at times. So I took an old friend's advice and started doing twenty pushups and twenty sit-ups multiple times in a day. Though it was hard at first and I could manage only ten each time with three rotations daily; to my surprise, I found that I was getting a quick workout in minutes and it gave me a boost and a fast heartbeat. I felt motivated without taking an extensive break or calling it a day. After the short exercise routine, I was ready to focus and continue studying. I repeated this every time I was tired. Eventually I started doing three sets of thirty in a day. I start with one set first thing in the morning and the remaining sets done during my study period. This also helped with backaches that I was getting by sitting down for so many hours in front of a computer screen.

Within a month, I was well into my exam preparation working out as I studied. Many times, when I wanted to get motivated, I would drop to the floor and attempt thirty to forty pushups. Within minutes, I was back on track and my mind was as sharp as it could be.

Give this a try if you can, but please take your physician's advice in case you have any health issues--this is what worked for us. Once you get hooked on to this exercise routine you may want to continue even after you pass the CCNA exam. By the way, this routine doesn't require any machines or club memberships or any additional cost to your CCNA budget. So you can do this anytime and anywhere you feel appropriate, just avoid doing this in public areas as you may be getting some extra unwanted attention. With regular workouts, you can have a CCNA and a six pack☺.

What We Did

As we mentioned earlier, you are subjecting your body, mind and family to stress that you may not have faced before. As a result, you may start eating more or develop new unhealthy habits. In my (Dean) case, I started eating a lot of junk food that resulted in me gaining weight.

Weight gain varies for different people, but the key here is to be aware of this and know how to deal with it. Give yourself a break every so often, especially when you feel overwhelmed. In order to build our stamina and mental focus, we started eating healthier by bringing fruits and vegetables to our weekend study location instead of the usual coffee and donuts.

Do not sweat it if you fall off the wagon with your diet, or miss your regular food and exercise routine at times. You will be able to get back on your old routine once you have the certification, and can tighten your belt later!

Another factor that you need to take into consideration is your environment and that it is suitable for your needs. You need to make sure that you are free from distractions, noises, and that the temperature is comfortable. We found the best environment was in our local office. On weekends, there were no disturbances since nobody would be there. It was nicely lit and had ergonomic furniture in familiar surroundings. Plus, we had a projector to watch and analyze our technical VoD on a big screen. Many times when we decided to take a quick break, Dean started his workout routine of pushups and sit-ups.

CHAPTER 28: WHAT TO DO IN THE LAST THREE WEEKS, DAYS AND HOURS

Preparing your moves

By this chapter, you should have already prepared and selected the best strategy for studying. There is a lot of information that is sprinkled in the previous chapters and we wanted to reiterate some of the key points in this chapter.

You should have registered for the exam three to four weeks prior to the targeted exam date. After doing that, it is very important to connect all the dots as to how the various networking technologies come into play with one another. It does not matter whether you are taking the ICND1 and ICND2 route or the single exam route for CCNA; by now, you should not only be familiar to with books and its chapters, but should also be comfortable in starting up your lab simulator and doing your labs. This means that you should be familiar with the CISCO IOS command structure.

Before attending a class you should have read and completed the primary CCNA self-study book and/or watched the VoD, finalized your question sheet and written down areas where you have doubts (remember that your questions have to be precise and to the point). You should have had hands-on experience also. **The last two weeks of your preparation should be more exam-centric and more focused on filling in the knowledge gaps** in certain areas that you may feel need more work and practice. This is not a time to do more research and dig deeper into new technologies. You can do that later after you pass your exam.

The last week of this period should be set aside for your final exam. Preparing, reviewing your notes, or any content that you need. You may have already bought some exam preps, flash cards and other tools which you may want to go over to reinforce your knowledge.

If it is feasible then the last three weeks is also the right time to take an instructor led class or a boot-camp. We say this because some of these courses run for 10 days. You should also use the notes and questions you have prepared, since this is a perfect opportunity to ask the instructor and other student's questions.

When in class, make sure that you are asking specific questions. In case you don't understand the answer or the class is falling behind schedule, be ready to have one-on-one time with the instructor. It is noteworthy, that some instructors may not be fully comfortable or at ease to do a deep dive on certain topics (and I am not talking about question dumps, we are referring to the technologies). This could be because they may think that talking more about a technology may cause confusion for other students or may throw the class off schedule. In rare cases, it might be that the instructor may not have a lot of teaching and real world experience. It's important to know your instructor before you enroll in a class. A CCSI (Certified Cisco Systems Instructor) will be able to help you understand the challenges that you are facing and be able to break its issues up in such manner that will make sense to you even after the class and especially in real work situations.

Try and avoid any classes that are "death by PowerPoint". Make sure the class is interactive and lively.

When asking questions in class, make full use of the white board; drawing a diagram brings much more clarity to what you are saying. You see, in our industry we have our own networking language regardless of which country or language you may speak. When Dean was teaching in Moscow many students could read English but could not speak it fluently. However they could easily ask questions by drawing on the whiteboard, thus understanding all the technologies that Dean was teaching except for his jokes☺.

Three days prior to the exam, you should be reviewing questions, and handouts as well as the hints that the instructor gave in the class and preparing yourself mentally for the exam. For those of us who may not be used to taking exams, you will want to collect as much information as possible about the exam, the policies, the exam location and any other relevant information. For example it may be useful to know that when the question has a radio button, you are required to provide single answer compared to the checkbox when you have to select multiple answers.

Mental preparation is an integral part of this entire process. Three hours before the exam you will be using this mental preparation to keep yourself calm and composed in order to prepare yourself for success.

You should visualize yourself in the exam, as well as how you will answer the questions, how you will be writing important notes during the survey portion, such as a subnet chart or any items that you think would be of use at the time of the exam.

What Would We Do

The art of studying is something that each of us may have to learn on our own. As we understand it, there is no one equation that fits all. Each of us has to learn our own most effective way of studying and make use of the techniques that are most beneficial to us. For example when I read a technical book, I use many color pens, highlighters and I [(Dean)] underline any topic/sections with a brief notes next to paragraph. I also used post it notes to flag any areas in the book. I underline the most important aspects of the book, that way I just have to read the highlighted or underlined sentences when I look back and get the basic idea of how the protocols operate and what are the most important items that I need to take with me. I found that the colors really made things standout and because my notes are written clearly, they are easy to read. Although the book may appear to be beaten up in the end, it looked attractive to me because it reflected the amount of time and effort that I put into learning the content.

I have worked with those who take notes on their computers and reference it. These notes are the condensed version of the book or courseware and this is what they refer to all the time for exam preparation. Regardless, the point is to learn the topics whichever way works best for you.

CHAPTER 29: THE LANDING

Test Day

On the day of your exam, arrive at the testing center at least fifteen to twenty minutes early. Give yourself enough time to take care of any traffic or unexpected delays that you may encounter. Bring two forms of ID. You may be requested to fill in your profile and your picture may be taken. You are not authorized to bring anything to the exam. You may be given some dry erase paper and a marker and are expected to give them back to the proctor once the exam is done. **Be cool, calm and collected during the exam.** You may not go back to any questions to reevaluate your answer. Be confident about your knowledge and walk into the exam with a clear and sharp mind so you can handle anything that anyone throws at you.

Prior to the start of the exam you will be given a survey to fill in. Though this is optional, you should take this time to write down any reference information that you think may help you to answer questions such as subnet chart in case you use one.

It's natural to be a bit nervous as the exam environment in general is very serious and can be stressful, but remind yourself that you need to concentrate on what is ahead of you. Tell yourself that it is okay to be nervous; this gives you the edge that you need to pass the exam. Remember that regardless of how you do in the exam, it's going to be over. Good or bad, it will be over. You need to know that even if you don't do well, during the exam you should collect your thoughts and do your best

As for the exam, you need to know that some of the answers may not be very obvious when you first read the question. You may have to read some of the questions three to four times and get inside of the mind of the question maker in order to interpret it correctly.

Knowing how to think like them and how you should be interpreting the questions may be your ticket to pass the exam.

What Would We Do

We always reach the exam venue at least thirty to forty minutes early. I [(Vivek)] get impatient when I reach too early so I always take my book along and read it in the car while waiting. About 15 minutes before the scheduled time I enter the exam center and am in front of the computer taking my test on time.

Once inside I take a few minutes to calm myself down, a few deep breaths and make myself comfortable. Only then, I start looking at the screen and start the exam. Although I have not done so, I have seen few candidates use earplugs to make sure that they are not disturbed.

CHAPTER 30: THE HOUR AFTER LANDING

You just came out of the exam; you have seen the actual questions and can assess yourself. If you have passed, then CONGRATULATIONS! Now you may start thinking about your reward and potentially your next certification. You should also perhaps look at Chapter 38 and Chapter 39 dealing with resume writing and interview preparation.

If you did not pass, then regardless of what is going in your mind, or how you feel about the exam, you should set your emotions aside and reflect on your experience. Please note that this is not easy. You may want to sit somewhere quiet and take some mental notes about what you did and what you can improve upon. This is crucial to your success. These mental notes will come in handy as you contemplate and reflect back. Although you might be feeling down, it is important to know that this is the time to probe your mind for all the areas of improvements and doubts while everything is still fresh in your mind. **We strongly advise you to not turn your cell phone on at this time**. Make your notes mentally and/or on paper before you begin talking to your family and friends.

Since both of us have so much going on in our minds and can be forgetful, we always have a pen and paper handy. We write down anything that comes to our minds at all times; this helps keep us on track and may work for you as well. At times, the solution to a problem may present itself in the most unusual way.

Usually after an exam we would write down everything that we can remember in short sentences or even a few words for every technology. We would then expand on these later on to make them more descriptive. This proved very advantageous to us.

What Would We Do

After taking the actual exam, it is imperative to reflect and evaluate yourself without any distractions. If we did not pass the exam we would feel a bit dejected and even depressed. In spite of that, we would plan to spend about an hour to reflect on the exam. The first thing we would do is to write down all the areas of technologies that were hard for us to understand or appeared confusing. Combining the above information with the exam result would give us a good idea about the areas of improvement. Based on this we will have a fair idea about how much more time we need for preparation for the next attempt.

All of this adds up to formulate an action plan that we can implement to achieve our CCNA. It is of utmost importance that booking your next attempt is an early part of your action plan.

CHAPTER 31: THE LAYOVER

Many engineers failed more than once

There is always a possibility of more than one attempt. It's alright if you failed the exam. Failure is part of any success, and a necessary part of life. The harsher the winter is, the more joyous and colorful the spring. It's the snow and cold winter that makes us appreciate the spring so much. Hardship and failure are a part of any successful journey. **Trying again is what distinguishes a halfhearted effort compared to a whole hearted effort.** It also identifies the traits of someone who wants, compared to someone who achieves. It's exactly for this reason that people walk away from certifications like CCNA; if it was easy everyone would get their CCNA. There are engineers that go through these tests two times, three times and more; it does not matter how many times you failed. What will matter is that you passed and no one in any interview will ask you about your number of attempts to pass your CCNA.

The point being, we all have to start somewhere and CCNA is a great place to start and **continue your journey to develop the necessary skills that any network engineer must have.** Not passing the CCNA exam is just a bump in the road, as we have indicated earlier in Chapter 30 "The hour after landing". Once you are done with the exam, you need to write down the areas that you felt you need more study on and then add them to the topics on which you see a low score on the exam result sheet. For the next day or so you need to create a plan in your mind as to how you are going to tackle those items either with your study partner, mentor or on your own.

What Would We Do

Both of us had to take some of these exams more than once. I [Vivek] would be absolutely disappointed and feel bad about not passing, and it happened to both Dean and I. The first time I [Vivek] took the CCNA beta exam with the simulation question I failed it because I was not used to scrolling and typing the exact syntax in a CCNA exam. Of course I was disappointed. On top of that there were no tools like PACKET TRACER to practice. However I did learn from that and got myself some hands on time on real network gear using decommissioned network devices and spares at work.

Try and follow Dean as an example. Dean has multiple certifications such as CCNA, CCDA, CEH, CCNP, CCSP, CCDP, and CCIE. Many of these require one or more exams and some of them like CCIE need a complete 8 hour lab. In Dean's case he failed his CCDA (Cisco Certified Design Associate) not once, but twice—on both occasions he felt very discouraged. After failing the second time he went directly to the bookstore, to see if he was missing something. He had studied the book and knew it inside out. Once at the bookstore by reviewing the books he realized that Cisco Press book was more in line with the blueprint of the exam then the alternative books. He bought the Cisco Press book and the third time was the charm!

The key point is that our spirit was not broken by temporary failures and we persevered to achieve all of these certifications. Can you imagine if Dean had stopped trying at his first failure? He would not have had all these certifications and we would all be missing a great teacher.

CHAPTER 32: REPOSITION YOURSELF

Shake it Off

First and foremost, you should feel proud of where you are and what you have accomplished. Only a few engineers will go this far and attempt to challenge themselves with something like this. Regardless of how you did, you have attempted to jump start your career and improve your life and that of your family. Failure is part of any organic process and without it, we would not appreciate the task ahead. It gives real meaning to "hard earned" once you pass CCNA. This is the price of success, which you should be willing to pay regardless of the number of attempts. Do not drop the ball now, continue moving forward, learn the lesson that you need to learn and shake it off. Do not let any setbacks stop you from reaching for your dreams.

It is natural that you may feel frustrated since you have invested months of your time with no solid results. But you need to look at your goal of getting your CCNA Certified Status. Not passing the exam is just another bump in the road and a small setback that you will not even remember after passing your CCNA exam. Do not even think about walking away from it. **You need to give yourself a 24-hour break and then evaluate yourself objectively**. Use the disappointment to fuel your hunger and determination to get your CCNA. This is the time to read that list you made in Chapter 1 "Are you ready to be a pilot" and remind yourself of all the good things that will come and what matters to you the most. Think of the prize you set for yourself in Chapter 13: "Reward for your successful flight". This is also when your inner circle (See Chapter 11 "Building your flight crew") will give you all the support and help you recover faster.

Find the areas that you need to improve upon. Your inner mind will tell you the doubts you have, so write all of them down. Combine these with the ones you had written in Chapter 30, "The hour after landing". Once written, you will see that what seemed like an uphill task in your mind looks achievable now. You can easily conquer them in a very short time. If others have achieved this, you can do the same.

The problem is that we are sometimes our own worst critic. **Do not get discouraged; shake off the negative thoughts** and think of the fame, respect, monetary rewards and bright future that you will have. Your attempt has told you that the CCNA is not impossible and after this experience, you should feel empowered and ready to use this to your advantage.

Once you start reviewing your material you may recognize that some of the questions are very similar to that from the actual exam. You will also realize that **CCNA is never about memorizing the questions but about understanding and applying technology to solve problems**. You will also know the importance of doing hands on labs. All those labs that involved configuration of router hostname, setting speed and duplex on ports to configuring routing protocols help you in passing your exam.

What Would We Do

If you don't pass the first time, try not to be disappointed, you are no less than any other person. Think to yourself, why am I disappointed? The answer lies within me. I will think and write down the technologies or topics that puzzled me in the exam. I will make a list until I cannot think of any more items that stopped me from passing this exam. This list should include all of the technical topics, as well as non-technical items like the need for more uninterrupted time for study, more time on Saturdays and Sundays or even studying at the library or office instead of home to avoid interruptions. Once I make my first list, I usually have a few more things to add to the list in the next 48 hours. I will keep on doing that until I am confident that I have noted all or almost all the items and topics that are stopping me. Then I will tally this with my exam result sheet.

This combined list becomes my road to success. I will immediately implement the corrections for the non-technical points like studying more on Sundays at the library to ensure that I can fully concentrate on the technical aspects. Now I will start studying the technical aspects in detail and try to use these in the lab if possible. I will ask for help from my mentor, friends or partner. I will pull out all the stops and study these topics till I am more confident. This time I will try to over prepare myself.

It has happened many times when I am practicing a topic in a lab or reading about it where I will remember that this is the type of question I was asked in the exam and if I was able to answer that or not.

Ideally, I will not wait for more than two or three weeks for the next round of the exams, but you should check Cisco's website for the amount of time (if any) you would have to wait. At the time of this book's publication you have to wait 5 days before you can retake the exam. However, if you are not feeling very confident a week before the exam, I would **postpone scheduling the exam for another week but only one time**. Do not keep on postponing it one week at a time for the next 3 months. If you have to postpone it twice then it means that either planning is bad or you are not following the plan accordingly. Follow the timeline.

Note: At present (Feb 2013) you can reschedule or cancel your scheduled exam 90 days before the exam date. After the 90 days you cannot change. Just in case you cannot be at the exam center on the scheduled date please call and let them know. Although you will forfeit your exam fee you will not be marked as a no show and you will be able to schedule your next exam immediately. If you are marked "no show" you will not be able to reschedule your exam for 30 days. Please check Cisco's website for the latest policy before making any decisions.

CHAPTER 33: THE NEXT FLIGHT

Keep it close

After your CCNA exam results, you have to put things into perspective as outlined in the last chapter. Give yourself one to two days per topic in which you think you need to improve or ramp up on. If your list for these topics is so long that it will take another two months then it means that your preparation for the first time was inadequate. However, this is rare and we usually recommend that you schedule and make your next attempt within three or a maximum of five weeks—again it depends on the retake policy which you must verify on Cisco's website.

When you come back from your exam, take one or two days off and then get right back to work. Do not break the momentum. This is a very important lesson that we learned the hard way. Think of your setback as a stepping stone. CCNA is exactly like what we described in Chapter 6 "How difficult is it?". It is difficult and challenging, but not impossible. All of your hard work has brought you this far, so continue to work on technologies that you think you could improve upon and would be to your benefit.

After one or two days of rest and recovery, you should start studying using any and all of the resources that you used for your preparation. Review the Video on Demand sessions and its notes; study the lessons that you think need attention after your last exam experience. **Contact your mentor and seek help.** Ask him or her for few minutes of their time and let them explain the concepts that you find difficult. If you have a partner, work with him/her as well. In case you have taken classes, there are some organizations that may allow you to retake the class free of charge. You may want to contact your training provider and even your instructor and ask for guidance as to how you can prepare better for the next attempt.

Don't get discouraged, as many engineers tend to walkway from these types of setbacks. Step-up with determination to pass the exam, run with the ball and carry it across the finish line. If you walk away from it now, this task becomes too large and it is human nature to ignore it and eventually quit all together.

Your focus at this time is to study the topics that you need to improve on. Don't spend too much time at the beginning on the topics that you are strong in. Go back to your daily studying schedule and try to work the plan. For some engineers, the use of flash cards may be a good review. Don't forget to go over the notes that you may have either the ones in the class or the ones that you took when reading or doing labs in the books with VoD. There are many sample questions in self-study books that you can use to test yourself.

If you keep on doing the necessary reviews and studying for the exam you may find out that even while sleeping, you are focusing on those topics or questions. You will also find that the tasks that were difficult the last time will now appear to be easier. Since you have experienced the actual exam once, you will be less nervous and more focused with greater concentration. Your silly mistakes and errors that caused you grief earlier will be miniscule now. In short, you will be humming along like a well-tuned engine. What used to be a marathon for you will appear like any other race.

What Would We Do

Both of us have had to take a certification exam a second time at one time or another. We did not have a book like this available to us at the time, but did use some of these techniques. Had we given up and not studied harder, we would not be CCIE's today and definitely would not be writing this book.

After following the process of making the list and reading, understanding and doing labs on the particular technologies, we would be ready to take the exam again. We would set our target date and book our exam slot with the nearest testing center.

We would visualize in our mind the steps we were going to take. Visualization will improve shortcomings and mistakes. For example, if I (Vivek) spent a lot of time on sub-netting questions the last time, I would make additional tables or notes on the sheet given to me at the testing center so that I can speed up. I will also make sure to look at the watch and time myself more carefully; maybe every 20 minutes (not after every question) to keep myself aware of my speed.

Since this is not the first time taking the exam I would not be nervous or panic when I see a question that I could not answer correctly. I will keep my cool, and depending on the time left I will not spend any more time than I can afford on one particular question.

The positive visualization, attitude and the planning that you can now do because of your earlier experience will surely help in making this attempt much easier.

CHAPTER 34: DO'S

This chapter encompasses all of those little things that may seem insignificant, but are extremely beneficial to follow for the CCNA exam.

1. Select **one to three mentors to help you** with your CCNA certification and to understand the technologies, how they are implemented in the production network. These mentors are there to help you. Ask them nicely and be considerate of their time. Many organizations have mentor programs, so you may want to join them or ask some of the engineers on the network team to work with you and allow you to shadow them; especially during maintenance windows which are at off hours when they have approval to make production changes during those hours.

2. The use of "?" (help) in Cisco IOS is your friend and enemy at the same time. If you are using help "?" during the initial learning phase then it is ok. Otherwise it usually means that you need more practice.

3. The use of help "?" (help) Cisco IOS after mastering a technology is recommended only when you try to go into different levels in a particular command group and try to find the options available.

4. Nowadays, everyone uses DYNAMIPS/GNS3, PACKET TRACER or some other tool for lab simulation because of its convenience. It is good for training but do practice on real devices also. Working on a real device is a different feeling. For example, you may notice

the difference in time when you do a "wr mem" (saving configuration) or the reload times. Many hardware specific features can only be tested on real devices.

5. Make sure to visit your training provider's forums and support group. Many questions are answered just by reading what others have posted.

6. If you prefer to join mailer lists or other CCNA study sites, please join, but make sure you don't get mired by the many "what if" scenarios people post. Sometimes a simple technology, such as duplex mismatch, can drag on and many questions can be raised. Each person has his own style of learning and I am not saying what others are posting is wrong. Some conversations are informative and could help with your exam. But if you have a limited amount of time then knowing the ins and outs of how automatic speed and duplex is negotiated deep down to the voltages, is not recommended.

7. Another very helpful thing is to teach a particular topic to a friend or a partner. When you teach a particular topic, you ask yourself a lot of questions and you usually master it yourself. If you can't do that, just make a video and post it on YouTube. The preparation itself will make you master the topic. (A word of caution here that the idea is to understand the technology and not spend time in making sure that you look good on YouTube).

The non-technical do's.

1. If you are sensitive to room temperature, take a jacket with you to the exam center. You will be sitting for 90 minutes and you might start feeling cold.

2. Get used to sitting for three to four hours at a time with full concentration on studying.

3. Register for the CCNA exam based upon the best time that you prefer and during a period of time that you can totally commit to it. I say this because you can choose the venue of your choice depending on whether you are an early morning or a late morning person and which exam time slot suits you. Do not try to squeeze the CCNA exam during lunch time or between meetings, because you don't want your mind focused on going back to the office by a particular time or about the next meeting. Your mind should be focused on passing the exam and be ready to hear all those congratulatory messages for your great achievement. (consider taking a day off)

4. Decide when you are going to study for a CCNA certification, and announce it. I have seen engineers hide this fact. Don't do that. As soon as you announce this to the world your mind will be committed and start working towards making this happen. For us, friends and family were ready to help. We got a lot of support in many forms, like getting more time to study because family took

work away from us, technical help on specific topics from friends, and good tips like the ones we have in this book.

5. Stretch your limits get uncomfortable and step out of your comfort zone. Only then new doors will open and opportunities will come. If you have never studied for 4 to 5 hours straight then this is the time to do it. Remember that the little bird has to make all of the effort in the world to break the egg shell to come out of it, but once it is out, it realizes how much bigger the world is.

6. Use your troubleshooting skills in labs when you are not getting the right results. Troubleshooting is both a science and an art. The science part is the logic used for honing in to the area with the problem and the art part is to reach the most probable cause without going through all of the iterations. What I mean is that if the light bulb in your room is not turning on, you do not go through all the steps (iterations) like

   a. Is there power available?

   b. Is the switch turned on?

   c. Is the wire connected at the switch?

   d. Is the wire connected at the other end where the bulb is connected?

   e. Has the bulb gone bad?

   Instead of going through all of this you turn the switch on and if the bulb does not light up you suspect the bulb right away. Why?

Because in your experience you have seen that a bulb goes bad most of the time.

Similarly once you have done a lot of labs and have understood the technology you will start to troubleshoot and get to the root cause of an issue much faster.

7. Make sure you are studying in a very comfortable environment. By environment we mean a place where there is good lighting, comfortable temperature, ergonomic furniture and other things like coffee, tea, paper, a printer, pens, a whiteboard, etc.

8. During your exam, you need to be focused. A little nervousness is okay, but if you are panicking you should remind yourself that this exam like many things is life will be over and within next 90 minutes or so. Whether you pass or fail, it will be history just like everything else in our lives

9. Bring some ear plugs if you feel you may get distracted by other noises, such as the fan or AC or other individuals in the room taking the exam. Remember that other individuals who are taking the exam may be nervous too. It is not unusual to see people talking to themselves or at times reading some part of the question aloud.

10. Wear comfortable clothing during the exam

11. Expect the unexpected; be alert and sharp. In case you read a question and don't understand it, you may want to re-read it. If you are still having issues try to remove all of the extra information

and rephrase the question in your mind in just a few words or a short sentence. Read and analyze the answers in case of multiple-choice; there may be a clue in there.

12. Do not treat every question the same. Some questions are easy and the examiners intend for it to be that way. Others may have a similar point but may take more time such as simulations. If answers to the questions come easily to you, then answer it and move forward. Don't waste time analyzing the answers which you already know.

13. On the day of the exam get to the site 30 minutes early and:

    a. Bring two forms of picture identification cards for example driver license and passport.

    b. Review any notes that you have taken and make a mental note as what you need to write down once you are in the exam room

    c. Prior to the start of the exam you may be asked to fill up the survey which will not reflect on your exam score. We normally use this time to write down on the laminated paper which the proctor provided all the notes and reminders such as the subnet charts or other important factors that you may feel might be of any help during the exam. This way, you don't use precious exam time for just writing a subnet chart or other important things that you think will help you in your exam. All the papers will need to be given back to the proctor once you are done with the exam.

    d.   If you are doing well, don't get excited or overconfident and start making silly mistakes. Be in control and monitor your time accordingly. If you are not doing well, don't get discouraged, you are in the exam room and are seeing the exam first hand. Analyze every question and answer them to the best of your abilities. Make mental notes on the areas that you need to ramp up on.

14. You will get your exam results within a few seconds of ending the exam. Believe me when we say that those are the longest seconds that you will see in your life. It happens to me even to this day after taking so many exams. Later the exam facilitator will provide you with a printed copy of your results. The score on individual topics in the exam is a roadmap for you to improve irrespective of whether you passed the exam or not. If there is a low score in routing protocols then you do need to read more, even if you passed the exam otherwise you will have problems on the job or when you start your CCNP.

CHAPTER 35: DON'TS

This chapter encompasses all those little things that may inhibit your progress and prevent you from passing the exam.

1. Don't go and just attend a boot camp and then attempt the exam. In our experience, it has worked for very few individuals. A friend of mine tried that approach and realized how much he didn't know and needed to study after the boot camp. If you are prepared, take the boot camp at the end of your studies just a few weeks before your scheduled exam date.

2. As we have told you, throughout this book, do not discuss any details of your exam with anyone. Neither in person, online, or with your instructor. If you divulge any of this you are putting yourself and the other person at risk. Check the Cisco website for detailed policies regarding non-disclosure agreements (NDA).

3. Use a standard generic keyboard. I ^(Vivek) had this problem when I went for one of my certifications. I was using a fancy portable Bluetooth keyboard at home. In my exam, I had a generic standard keyboard and that slowed me down. You don't want to press the enter key by accident instead of the shift key and move to the next question.

4. As we have mentioned in Chapter 34 "Do's", it is a good idea to join CCNA study groups, but if there is a lot of gloom and doom type of personalities in a particular group; avoid them. You don't

need their negative energy; this will only slow you down. If you join a crowded study group, you may not get your questions answered. Some groups are great for networking and relationship building. If you are looking for a good study partner, you may look at these study groups as a vehicle to find your study partner. Therefore, use them as a guiding tool.

5.   In our experience, two or a maximum of three is a good number of partners. Having a group of five or more does not really work out. There are always exceptions and our advice is based on our experiences only. In CCNA certification, we consider partnership an optional path; we prefer having mentors first and then perhaps the consideration for partner should come next.

6.   Brute force method. What we mean by this is that you go and take the exam five or six times and remember all of the questions. By the seventh or eighth try you will be able to pass. BRUTE FORCE DOES NOT WORK. There are no shortcuts to a CCNA and if you manage to pass by brute force then you are just a paper certified and it won't get you far in your career. So it doesn't matter how you look at it brute force does not work.

7.   Do not refer to or read exam dumps. This is the worst thing you can do to yourself. You may ask why? Here are some reasons
You will not understand the topics and technologies and as a result you will have:

- Very low confidence in yourself that you will ever be able to solve a real networking issue.

- You will be failing many interviews because you will not understand or know the technologies. Believe me it takes just the first two or three questions to know if the candidate has a paper certification or really deserves to be called a CCNA

- Every time you are congratulated on passing your CCNA and asked the question; "how did you do it", you will either tell the truth about using an exam dump which will negate your sense of accomplishment or make up an elaborate lie about studying.

- Exam dumps do not allow you to learn and thus when trouble shooting issues come up your only input is what you memorized. This could at times make you look like an individual that lacks real understanding of the technology required.

CHAPTER 36: SKY IS THE LIMIT

CCNA Success

The world of networking is different from the world of end users; without a network there is no meaningful end user application. This also means that majority of other IT teams and users are our customers. We have to adhere to their needs. For example, an email server meltdown could be catastrophic, but the impact is nothing like the entire network meltdown, which would not just impact the mail server but all other services and communication like voice and video. The point being, we need to realize the importance of our service and the impact to customers.

You will not get rewarded when the network is up, but you will get noticed once it is down; some compare networking with the plumbing or the telephone at home; you will notice it mostly when these services breakdown.

Experience does help with your career and the knowledge that you bring to the table. Although experience is recommended, it is not a must, to obtain your CCNA certification. Having some experience of course would be beneficial. Once you have accomplished your goal, you should reward yourself. A family trip, taking a cruise, getting that latest mobile phone or tablet computer, getting that piece of jewelry or watch that you have been looking at is now a possibility. You will also find that you have so much time, especially in the evenings or weekends, that you can catch-up with friends and family activities.

One thing to always keep in mind is that just because you are certified doesn't mean that you should sit back and do nothing. **Continuous learning is part of the process, so seek out new ways to learn and grow; don't stay stagnant; follow through and pursue other goals and certifications.** As we say in Chapter 5 "CCNA flight/career path", CCNA will launch you to the networking world. **CCNA is like that bullet train** that will take you faster and get you there quicker, compared to another normal train. Within the span of three short years you have to recertify your CCNA, by taking the written test either for the composite exam or by taking other exams which would recertify your CCNA and move you up to an advanced professional certification. In other words, you have to get recertified every three years, so why not take some advanced exams and naturally move your skill and career further.

What Would We Do

The first thing we would do is to celebrate and get what we had visualized. Yes, there is a good reason to celebrate because CCNA was a tough challenge and we finally made it. All of the hard work and dedication has paid off. All of those nights that we spent struggling with technologies and working hard and researching on the internet, looking up YouTube videos and trying to simulate it in our lab to learn, has paid off handsomely. We know that we not only got our CCNA certified status, but that we *deserve* it.

We would inform our boss and upper management that we have achieved this certification and tell them that we are ready to take the next challenge. We would also ask our boss about the company sponsoring some part or all of my further studies like CCNA specialization or CCNP.

We would tell all our friends and lastly we would start thinking ahead as to how to use our stamina for studying and our confidence to understand technologies and pass more exams to further our career. We would choose from a CCNA specialization in Security, Voice, Service Provider, Video or we would go for CCNP in one of the chosen tracks. We would also set a target date for this and start studying.

CHAPTER 37: YOUR FLIGHT PLAN

Timeline for CCNA Preparation

If you are reading this chapter just after reading one or two other chapters in this book, you may not understand clearly what we are suggesting to do in different parts of a timeline. It is recommended that you read the book completely so that you may take full advantage of these strategic timelines. These timelines are there to give you direction, but the pace has to be adjusted according to your style and situation. We are showing you the map, the path to take but it is for you to decide the speed and the stops along this path. In this chapter there are three distinct timelines; **two for the dual exam (ICND1 and ICND2) track and one for the single composite exam track.**

While Dean and I were discussing the making of a timeline for completing CCNA we could not complete this in one or two or even four sittings. The reason was that there is so much to learn especially for someone who is new to networking. Add to that the multiple ways of learning like Video on Demand (VoD), Audio on demand, reading books, attending an online class or attending a live class and it becomes very complex to present all these options in a particular order in a definite timeline. Each individual has their own way of learning and it is usually a mix of reading the book, watching Video on Demand, working with your mentor or partner and a few more resources like reading articles on the web and watching an informative YOUTUBE video.

Keeping all of the above in mind we finally came to a timeline that we thought will prepare you for your CCNA challenge.

For ICND 1 we decided to prepare a daily and weekly schedule.

For ICND 2 we prepared weekly schedules only because we assumed that by passing the ICND 1 exam you will know your study style and you will be able to make your daily schedule easily from the weekly ones. There will be times when you will have to make finer adjustments to your study schedule and that is alright. Making those finer adjustments will give you the feel for your studying style, and will also help you in studying for future exams.

In our teaching experience both Dean and I have seen that some engineer's like to read the book and then watch the Video on Demand while some engineers watch the Video on Demand and then read the book, however most of them have a blended style of learning that mixes VoD, reading the book and doing labs. It all depends on what you prefer. So we decided to allocate time for VoD and labs but we did not give it a fixed place in the schedule. We left it up to you to use the hours allocated for VoD to the best of your own study style.

Lastly we also put some slack time in both the schedules for ICND 1 and ICND 2. This slack time is there so that you can absorb the loss of time due to unknown emergencies without going off the schedule.

Two Exam – MACH 1 timeline

This is a timeline that is made specifically for someone who is starting there CCNA certification journey. This timeline is suitable for a number of individuals who want to study and learn networking.

- You may be someone who is interested in networks and have decided to learn and take this certification

- You could be someone who has been dealing with the physical installs of the network and want to learn more and move ahead in your career

- You can be someone who has been working in other related technical fields like communications in the army or handling cable and DSL infrastructure

- You might be someone who has come to the conclusion that due to technological changes in the company you have to learn networking and upgrade your skill set else you may will not be working much longer in the position of your choice.

Whatever your reason we are going to give you a framework below which will lead you to being a CCNA at a comfortable pace, where **you can be in a fulltime job and still study for your CCNA**. This timeline is based on the 2 exam track and will take less than 8 months to complete. This time is approximate and it is you who can speedup or slowdown the pace according to your study situation and environment.

ICND1

Day 1 to Day14 (14 Days)

Before you start your CCNA journey we want you to take 2 weeks to prepare yourself. This includes not only preparing yourself by setting up a study schedule and catching up on your sleep but also putting together all the right resources for your un-interrupted study. These resources can be

1. Exam preparation books and reference books.

2. Computer and other hardware to do your labs.

3. Software that will facilitate you with doing labs.

4. Decide on the courseware / training material to use.

5. Video on demand course.

6. Miscellaneous materials like pens, colored pencils, notebooks, highlighters, sticky notes etc.

7. Bookmark websites that have helpful resources for our studies.

8. "YOUTUBE" channels and Videos that explain a variety of technologies.

This is by no means an exhaustive list of resources but is a good start for you. Please use this time to gather whatever in your mind is the best suited to make you successful. You may ask me that since you are so new to networking how you can possibly know what is best suited for you? We would say that if you would want to try something entirely new like for example climbing a mountain peak, you will surely not wake up on a

Sunday and just start climbing. If you want to be successful you will probably find out facts like

- How high is the peak?

- How much time does it take for a first time climber like you?

- How will be the weather on the day you want to climb?

- You will probably want to talk to someone who has already earned their certification and gone through it. (A mentor).

- You would also do some preparation like exercising to have more stamina to complete the climb.

- You would also learn to use the tools needed in a successful climb and possibly take some sort of a class or have someone guide you for it.

Similarly for doing your CCNA you will have to do the basic ground work and find out what is suitable for you. If you get a good training provider and mentor (good coach to teach you how to climb) you will be on the right track much faster. For some candidates 2 weeks will be too much time and for some it will not be enough. In our view with a little guidance from your mentor and your own research 2 weeks should be enough for you to set yourself on the path of learning which guides you to success.

Using the above mentioned resources we suggest using a daily and weekly timeline. After reading the timeline below you may ask us as to how does this cover all the learning objectives for ICND 1 and ICND 2 as per Cisco's website? Our answer to that would be that as stated earlier this time line is a framework or a map to being a CCNA. We assume you will be using at least one book written specifically for ICND 1 and ICND 2 exam. This could be a CISCO PRESS book or could be a book from another publisher. Whatever is your choice it should cover all the learning objectives at the depth necessary for CCNA. We did not want to list each and every learning objective here and give you un-necessary detail. We rather wanted to give you a framework of guidelines that is sufficiently specific so that you can clearly chart your own path thus giving you the flexibility and command of your own success.

This timeline is 100 days (about 13 weeks) and can afford 4 days of slack time. This timeline also has 14 days allocated exclusively for studying using Video on Demand and 11 days of lab time.

Note: *A day of study is 3 to 4 hours on a weekday and 7 to 8 hours on the weekend (about 29 to 36 hours per week).*

Network Fundamentals   Week 3

Day 15 to day 21 (7 days)

This is the week when you pick up your book and move ahead in your journey that will take you far ahead in your future. So tighten your belt and get ready to zoom ahead. Like any other journey there will be bumps in the road and there will be traffic jams and at times the road will be so bad that it will be hard to travel. Sometimes you will get bad directions or you will be lost, but all of this is expected and you should be ready to deal with the unexpected.

Know from the start that as you move forward there will be topics and terminology that will be hard to grasp and at times there will be topics that will be very hard to understand. If you are driving and see a big pothole on the road, do you stop? No, you don't. You cleverly avoid it. Similarly if you see a topic or a technology that is kind of hard to understand, make a note of it or mark it in your book and think about what part you understand and what you don't. Think about what question or questions you will have to ask to clarify this and write them down. Once you have written all of these questions down keep moving ahead.

This technique, though simple, has helped me (Vivek) conquer a lot of technologies and will help you too.

Now what happens if you are driving and see a huge obstacle in front of you? You have to drive around it or get out, and climb over it and keep moving on. You need to do the same for a topic that you cannot understand at all. Even after doing two CCIEs, there are times where I (Vivek) am not able to grasp a new technology and have to work around it for the time being and then either get the help of an expert or read about it and do research. Hands on labs can also help you get a much better understanding.

You get the idea by now. Keep reading and keep moving. There are times when topics were not very clear in the earlier chapter become very clear after reading the next one. Each one of us has our own style of learning. Some of us read fast to get the lay of the land and then come back and read slowly but thoroughly to absorb the technologies and topics. I (Vivek) am like that. However, Dean reads it very slowly but is very thorough. So by the time I have finished a book, he is done with only the first 3 or 4 chapters. But he knows those chapters completely and to tell you a secret here, there have been times where I just skimmed through the first few chapters of the book because I knew that I could ask Dean about those any way and get a very detailed answer.

Another approach that both Dean and I love is visual learning. We learn a lot by watching Video on Demand using the technique discussed in chapter 25.

Whenever I go out to eat in a new restaurant I really don't understand what all those fancy words in the appetizer menu mean. If available I usually order the sampler tray. This is a tray that has a small portion of almost all the appetizers that are being served. This way I can choose my top 3 or 5 appetizers and order one now and the rest in my future visits to this restaurant.

Consider Week 1 of ICND 1 like that sampler tray. This week gives you a taste of all the major technology topics that you will be reading in the weeks ahead. Like the example of the restaurant you may choose what you like the best and read that first but unlike the restaurant you will have to read them all and master them all. You cannot leave one or two aside after reading a few pages.

Since this week is devoted to introducing you to the terms and technologies of CCNA, you will be reading a lot of unfamiliar words and acronyms. These being all theoretical concepts it may become a bit monotonous. When I [Vivek] started reading this, there were times where I dozed off. I used to ask myself how this theoretical OSI model was going to help me in maintaining networks. Little did I know that it does help you, so make sure you don't skip over it? Read it and try to make it fit into some sort of a logical way in your mind.

Day 15

This day should be used to go over the basics of computer networking and the OSI Model. Pay special attention to the layers of the OSI model and what Protocol Data Units (PDU's) are called at layer 2 and layer 3. Read this and understand this to the best of your knowledge and take some rest. Watch the VoD if any. Spend some time thinking of this model and try to conceptualize it in your mind.

Day 16

On this day you start reading about IP Addressing. You will learn that IP Address is the identification for network devices which is similar to a name for us humans. This is one of the logical topics and you will be able to read this easily. There will be some bumps in the road as you have to relate this to OSI model. You may have some questions but read patiently and move ahead.

Day 17

This is the day that you learn all about your LAN technologies. You learn terms like CSMA/CD and Ethernet, 10 base 2 and 10 base T, twisted pair and so on. You will become familiar with Hubs, switches and different types of cabling. As you are cruising along dealing with full duplex and half duplex you are suddenly given this not so easy concept of Ethernet Frames. This seems a bit intimidating but if you look at it logically it makes sense.

Day 18

After the LAN technologies it's the WAN technologies. These are very different from LAN because of the distances covered by these networks. These are the technologies that enable you to IM with a friend halfway across the world. You read about clock rates, frame relay, different types of WAN links and WAN protocols.

Day 19

Now that you have dealt with layer 2 and layer 3 it is time to talk about layer 4. That is TCP/IP. This is a nice protocol and you will admire its capabilities of error recovery and windowing and reordering of packets etc. This will lead you to know how this is used in real life with HTTP or DNS or how this layer is used for all the higher level software like Email or Instant Messaging. An understanding of this will also tell you how hackers use this layer to get unauthorized access. This also leads to how firewalls use this to protect networks. This chapter is a handful and should be read slowly or in a way that suits you. The idea is to absorb all the information in a slow and steady manner.

Day 20 and 21

If you have followed the above, you did great for your first week of studying. These two days will be used to revise these topics and watch the Video on Demand if any on these topics. This will solidify your concepts and remove many of the doubts that you had. This is also the time to get your questions answered from your mentor, colleague or post it on networking forums. Remember there is no silly question. Ask questions, but do ask in detail. Use the guidelines that have been stated elsewhere in the book. For example, instead of asking which routing protocol should I use for a medium sized organization you should ask "Should I choose EIGRP or OSPF for an organization with 150 Routers and switches with one campus building and 50 branch offices"?

Another word of caution is that you should use your favorite internet search engine to get answers before asking the question on online forums. Rely much more on answers from Cisco's forums than other sites. We don't mean to say that some other webpages will have wrong information. Some them have wonderful information not found anywhere but it is better to cross check it. Once you do this a number of times you will find your own reliable resources on the internet. You should not look ignorant by asking questions like what are the topics to study for CCNA when this is easily answered by searching for "CCNA exam topics" on the web.

Sub-netting   **Week 4 to 6**

Day 22 to 37 (16 Days)

These sixteen days are dedicated to learning sub-netting. I have put in two plus weeks here because almost everyone has told me that this is very difficult and on an average you need at least a week and half to understand. Many engineers perceive this is the most dreaded topic of CCNA.

If you ask me personally, this is a difficult concept to understand. When I [Vivek] was studying for my CCNA I struggled with it also for a very long time because I did not have a mentor. However when I figured it out after a long struggle, it was straightforward. I could do it in my head and people were amazed by that. Now-a-days there are a lot of web resources and videos dedicated to this topic and you can easily find these using your browser.

During these 16 days you can spend two days' worth (About 8 hours) of time watching Video tutorials and 14 days of time to read and practice the topic. After these 16 days you should be able to explain

What are the different classes of Ipv4 Subnets?

What is the difference between Class-full and Class-less networks?

What is a subnet mask?

How to read and interpret a network with its subnet mask?

How to design a network with subnets given a requirement?

How to find the Broadcast Address, The Subnet Address and the number of hosts in a particular IP Address and subnet mask pair?

LAN Switching   **Week 6 to 8**

Days 38 to 51 (14 Days)

This section rapidly builds on the concepts you already learned on day 17 of Network Fundamentals section. After reading about LAN switching for all of this week you should be able to answer all the questions you had earlier about LAN switching. This week will make a solid foundation for you about LAN Switching that will help you for the rest of your career so be patient and start reading. You need to read it first, then try and comprehend it. Once you understand it, you don't have to remember it. The earlier you do it, the better it will be for you.

Day 38 and 39

Learn about hubs, bridges and switches and the concept of how two or more hosts communicate on a network with each other. Understand how each of these work, and how this will lead to collision domains and broadcast domains. You will also learn about network loops and how to stop them with Spanning Tree Protocol. Pay attention to the concept of a VLAN also this is used everywhere now. If you are getting bored of reading all this fear not, as for next few days you will be doing a lot of hands on in your lab.

Day 40 and 41

This day is spent learning about Cisco catalyst switches. You will become familiar with one or more of the switch models and learn about its LED's. You will also learn

How to access a switch remotely or through a console port?

How to configure it and how to store the configuration?

How to erase a configuration?

How to go into different configuration modes?

How to help on the command line during configuration?

Day 42 and 43

This day leads you into more detailed configurations like

How to secure access to the switch using password security?

How to secure the password itself by password encryption?

How to configure Secure Shell (SSH) access?

How to configure Interfaces?

How to configure an IP Address on the switch?

How to secure ports on a switch?

How to configure VLANs?

What is the difference between NVRAM, RAM and Flash memory?

This is a day of fun. However, be cautious of one thing we have seen in many students. Typing in the commands is very easy; it is a 5 minute process. However, **understanding what each command is doing and checking and confirming** what you have done is working or not is slightly cumbersome. Take the long road. Here you have plenty of time. Practically doing these on a device or a simulator will solidify all of theories that you have been reading until now. This will give you confidence in your learning.

Day 44 and 45

These days are used for validation and verification of your configurations and troubleshoot the configuration in case of a problem. You will learn how to check the interface states and what each of the states mean. How to deal with speed and duplex issues? How to look at mac addresses and forwarding tables? Needless to say doing this as a lab will be absolutely helpful. So watch the VoD where ever possible and do it hands on.

Day 46 to 48

This day should be used to put everything that you have learned about LAN's into practical configurations. Go back and read the theoretical concept if need be. Watch the VoD if needed. All of hands on items should be completed. This should include basic and advanced configuration, verification and troubleshooting. This is where working with a partner helps you. You can configure and leave issues in it and let you partner troubleshoot it. You can quiz each other on the concepts and it is amazing how much and how fast you learn when working with a partner.

Day 49 and 50

It is amazing how much you have learned in about six weeks. You should feel empowered. Since you have been doing so much hands on this day can be used to hit the book again and learn about wireless LANS also. It is good to know about it anyways as you might be running one at home. Learn the different wireless standards, how each one is different from the other. Wireless security is an integral part of wireless LAN's and it should be read thoroughly.

Day 51

This is a free day. You can do whatever you want to on this day. Revise what you have done, just take a day off or start preparing for the week ahead.

Routing   Week 8 to 10

Day 52 to 66 (15 Days)

These two weeks are dedicated to Routing. Believe me this was real fun for me. I loved the concept of routing and how routers make life much easier and able to connect us globally. Although I am listing different sets of activities to be done on different days but for me all these merged together. In my case I (Vivek) read about the topics and then started configuration. So reading about the ports etc. led me to making a router connect to other routers and that led me to configure it. Once I am done configuring, I need to verify it using show commands and other commands. Of course I see problems and do need the troubleshooting to be completed.

Days 52 and 53

These two days are spent understanding the physical aspects of routers. The different ports and interfaces, the different LED's and how the physical connections are made to make it do its job. You will see a similarity in IOS commands between the switch and the router. This would be a good time to learn how to upgrade or downgrade IOS on a router and doing a password recovery. These days are interesting and very hands on.

Days 54 to 59

The hands on from the previous days, makes you hungry to learn about how this small box can do magic. This box gives you the power and makes you the master of how packets move through the router and how can these be directed as per your wishes or design.

You will learn about routing protocols and probably about RIP to start with. You can configure static and dynamic routing and use show commands and other commands to verify what you have configured.

Days 60 to 62

These days are for sharpening your troubleshooting skills. There are many commands in the Cisco IOS that let you do detailed troubleshooting. If you have understood the concepts that you read in Network Fundamentals section and the LAN switching section you will be able to see all of that in action and use ARP tables, MAC Address tables, Debugs and a variety of show commands to check your work.

It is fun to see and compare the output of various show commands when your setup is working and when it is not working. Make sure to note the symptoms that you see when there is problem as these will help you troubleshoot faster in future.

Check any troubleshooting scenarios that you can find in your book.

Days 63 and 64

This is a good time to watch any Video on Demand lessons or watch the Videos for the topics that you think you need to reread. In short these days are to be used to reinforce your newly acquired skills. Watch all of them and use what you learn by doing hands on labs.

Days 65 and 66

Some students finish this section early and take these days off. While others enjoy it so much that they can't get enough of it and keep trying different ways of configuration and keep breaking the network and see the effect of those on the various show commands.

This is also a good time to watch any Video on Demand lessons that you may have to reinforce your newly acquired skills.

WAN   **Week 10 to 12**

Day 67 to 78 (12 days)

This week builds on Day 4 of the first week.   I suggest that you read over all the chapters in you book this day. This will give you the breadth of technologies that are used in WAN. This will also give you an idea about the hands on labs that will be done for this topic. First read it and understand it completely. Then go for the hands on configuration.

Day 67 to 72

These six days are to be used for reading your book and watching the VoD for this topic. This section introduces you to Wide Area Network technologies like DSL, Cable, Modems, and WAN Circuits etc. It seems like numerous concepts, but once you understand one section, others will fall into place. This section will also cover NAT and PAT which is widely used even at a home router that connects multiple devices at home to the internet.

Day 73 to 77

These days are for hands on labs for WAN and if you are done early you can connect your LAN that you had configured last week to this WAN or make a mix of it that you think works for you and do hands on configuration and troubleshooting.

You should also refer to the Video on Demand lessons frequently as needed and use the technique that we suggested in Chapter 25.

Day 78

Take this as a rest day. Relax and reflect on what you have learned so far. You will realize that in a few short weeks you have an enormous amount of knowledge. Your mind will be racing with lots of ideas and techniques that you can try and learn.

Depending on how you feel about your preparation, now is the time to schedule your ICND1 exam. You can schedule this in the next two weeks' time. This should be enough time for you to prepare and revise all that you have done.

Final Section   **Week 12 to 13**

Day 79 to 89 (11 days)

This section is for you to sit down and revise all the topics especially the theoretical concepts. Start doing sample questions that came with your book, remember **it is not good enough to get the answer correct you should also know the reason why** it is so. It would be a good idea to go over each topic that Cisco expects you to know and see which ones need more work. See the VoD for those and read the relevant chapters in your book. Do hands on labs where applicable but do this till you remove all doubts in your mind.

This is the time when you could be attending your ICND 1 boot camp. The boot camp not only is a great revision but gives you immense confidence as you will have all your questions answered by the instructor and you will have lot of hands on labs completed too. The instructors cannot tell you about specific questions in the exam but pay special attention to where they stress learning of certain sections while they go easy on other sections.

Exam time   **Week 13 and 14**

Day 90 to 96 (7 Days)

You should be taking the exam during this time. If you pass great, you have moved ahead the first big step is behind you. In case you did not pass the exam don't worry. Check you exam results sheet and see what your areas of weakness are and come right back and start hammering them out. Don't wait and don't get dis-heartened. Failure is a precursor to success, so don't let this stop you (See Chapter 33 "The next flight"). A few months from now when you are a CCNA you will not be remembering this small event of not passing the exam in your first attempt.

ICND 2

This starts your next big and final step towards you being a CCNA certified engineer. With all the hard work you have put in for passing the ICND1 exam you have completed more than half your journey. More than half because the last time you started you had to prep yourself for 2 weeks before starting the actual exam preparation. This time you might not even need one day. You know your study style and will be able to make a schedule for yourself using our framework below with a greater ease and a very high level of confidence. You will be getting yourself into the same study schedule that you used for ICND1 and it will be very easy for you to allocate time and study with full concentration. As stated at the beginning of this chapter this study timeline has been broken down into weekly topics. The breaking down of the week's study into a daily schedule is left for you to decide according to your style. This should not be too difficult for you now as you have the experience from your ICND1 preparation. **This schedule is 137 days (about 19 weeks) long and has 5 days of slack time and has 14 days divided among the various sections for Video on Demand.** You can flexibly allocate the VoD time across the complete schedule as you deem fit.

ICND 2 is very technical and you have a lot to learn but try and think of it as fun. You will see that all the technical concepts you learned in ICND 1 are being taken to the next level and more twists and turns are being added to them. Initially it may seem very complex but fear not as much of this can be done in hands on labs and that makes it much easier to understand. Initially it may seem intimidating but believe in yourself and your knowledge of ICND 1. Anytime you feel overwhelmed refer back to the basics of that particular topic in your ICND 1 book. This is also the place where your mentor or partner can help you. However before you ask for help ask yourself, what questions you will ask. Try to make your questions as specific as possible. For example; Instead of asking I don't understand VLAN's you can perhaps ask yourself a series of questions like:

1. Why do we need VLAN's?

2. What are the advantages of having a VLAN?

3. What is a default VLAN?

4. How many VLAN's can we have on a Cisco switch?

Once you answer these questions you will know what part of VLAN's you don't understand and can ask a very specific question.

Another way to frame the question could be "I understand the following:

1. Why do we need VLAN's?

2. What are the advantages of having a VLAN?

But I don't understand:

1. What is a default VLAN?

2. How many VLAN's can we have on a Cisco switch?

3. How does a PC in one VLAN communicate with another PC in the same VLAN on the same switch or on a different switch"?

Framing of these questions will help you clear up a few of your own doubts itself and you will also tell your mentor that you respect his time and are not asking him to spoon feed you everything.

Enough with strategy, it is time to get to the schedule of ICND2.

Routing Protocols   **Week 1 to 5**

Day 1 to 32 (32 Days)

These days are dedicated to routing protocols and these were my favorite. I ^(Vivek) loved routing and learning about different routing protocols. All these routing protocols did the same job but in a different way. It was very interesting to note the differences between them and find out why these were made in to behave in a certain way. For example RIP sends routing updates more frequently than OSPF. Maybe this will generate lot of questions in your mind that you can ask your mentor or your colleagues.

Like all other study intervals this interval also ends with troubleshooting the different routing protocols that you have learned to configure. Almost everything that you study here can be done hands on in a lab so take your time and practice that.

Day 1 to 2 (2 Days)

Use these two days to further enhance the basic concepts of routing. A lot of reading but this will be your base for the next 30 days of adventure in routing protocols. I have divided these thirty days into three sections of

10 days each. Each one devoted to one routing protocol. Feel free to rearrange these according to your convenience. (Note: Just wanted to add for your knowledge that you are not required to read about IGRP now which was another Cisco proprietary routing protocol)

All these routing protocol sections require you to read your book, watch the VoD and then do the labs. If you are stuck use your troubleshooting experience from doing previous labs and do a step by step troubleshooting. Developing this habit of going logically step by step will save you a lot of heart burn when you are doing it under pressure on a live network.

Day 3 to 12 (10 Days)

Use these days to study the RIP protocol. This includes doing labs and knowing your show commands.

Day 13 to 22 (10 Days)

Use these days to study the EIGRP protocol. This includes doing labs and understanding the use of show commands.

Day 23 to 32 (10 Days)

Use these days to study the OSPF protocol. This includes doing labs and understanding the use of show commands.

Ask yourself at the end of this study section how comfortable do you feel about routing now. You should feel very comfortable. If not go back and read, watch VoD, ask your mentor and colleagues but be confident before you move to the next section.

Day 33 to 58 (26 Days)

The next 26 days of your ICND2 journey are dedicated to other forms of Routing like the concepts of Static routing and how to control routing and flow of traffic by using Route summarization and Access Lists. We have all heard the phrase "One size fits all" and we also know that this approach does not always work. There are exceptions to the rule and it is same for routing. There will be use cases wherein you are required to route traffic for all devices from a datacenter to the internet except for a select few devices. Another example is that only these 10 admin workstations are allowed to log on to network devices like routers and switches and 5 others are only allowed to log on to servers for administration. Whenever we have a situation like this access lists are used. Access Lists which are also called ACL's are of many different types and if not applied correctly can cause lot of problems. That means that you should not only configure these but also learn to troubleshoot this in case of a typo or any other errors. Needless to say VoD along with hands on labs will be needed to solidify the concepts and its uses in your mind.

Day 33 to 35 (3 Days)

After reading so much about the dynamic routing protocols you will learn that you can do without it by using static routes. However it is not practical to run a big network only on static routing. But this does not mean that it is not needed. Static routes are a part of any network.

Day 36 to 42 (7 Days)

These days are dedicated exclusively to different types of ACL's and how to use them. VoD and hands on lab is a must for this.

Day 43 to 50 (8 Days)

These days are dedicated to VLSM and Route summarization. These concepts go hand in hand and your expertise of sub netting will help you here. Hands on labs are a must. Do watch VoD.

Day 51 to 58 (8 Days)

These days are here to cover any other topics related to Routing and to practice and perfect your knowledge of routing and different ways you can affect routing using ACL's, route summarization and static routes.

WAN   Week 9 to 11

Day 59 to 76 (18 Days)

Learning about routing and routing protocols leads to the topic of WAN. Frame relay was an integral part of WAN's but is slowly being overtaken by newer technologies. However this is still there even in the CCIE lab. We keep on hearing rumors that this topic will slowly be replaced by more relevant technologies and why not. Cisco is in the forefront of technological development and it does a good job in keeping its Certifications updated but this also makes sure that all Cisco Certified engineers will learn newer technologies because they will have to pass the exam to keep their certification current. All other WAN related topics like Point to Point links, VPN etc. are to be completely finished by the end of this section.

LAN Switching   **Week 11 to 15**

Day 77 to 99 (23 Days)

The first few weeks of your ICND2 journey are dedicated to routing. These three weeks will make you competent to handle a major part of LAN tasks so read it, understand it, try it with a hands on lab to make sure that there are minimal doubts left after this period.

Two major topics in LAN switching are VLAN's and Spanning tree. These are not only fundamental but also cool concepts and almost every network depends on these. Needless to say these are always a part of your ICND2 exam and any interview that you will attend. There will be more switching related topics like trunks, ether channel and port security and all those are to be covered in this section.

Lastly once you understand it and know how to configure it you should also know how to troubleshoot it. VoD will surely help you in Spanning tree and there are many great Videos on YOUTUBE also by leading trainers on this topic.

When doing labs on spanning tree you will see if you have a configuration error which may create a loop in the network or if you do it on purpose you may lose connection to the equipment. So be aware of it and do it anyway. It is better to do this in a lab setting instead of a live production network.

IP Addressing   Week 15 to 17

Day 100 to 115 (16 Days)

Your interesting learning journey is nearing its end now. You have learned most of the technologies. All that is left is the IP Addressing. Although you did a lot about IP Addressing and sub-netting in ICND1 but ICND2 takes it a step further. This section addresses the problem with IP Address scaling using NAT or to use the latest and greatest IPv6. As of writing this book IPv6 is going towards a slow adoption and a good understanding of this will serve you for years to come. This section like any other section needs your full concentration and dedication to understand these topics.

As you come to the end of this section evaluate yourself. Depending on how comfortable you feel you should probably schedule your exam in the next 7 to 14 days.

Final Week   Week 17 to 18

Day 116 to 122 (7 Days)

This week is there for the exclusive purpose of revision and clearing up of any doubts if any. By the end of this week you should feel ready to take this exam. Practice and reread what you have learned. You will not only appreciate what you have learned but there may be doubts that will clear out in your mind as you bring together all the knowledge.

Try reading aloud or teaching a colleague any topics that you don't feel ready—remember teaching is learning.

This is the time when you could be attending your ICND 2 boot camp. The boot camp not only is a great revision but gives you immense confidence as you will have all your questions answered by the instructor and you will have lot of hands on labs completed too.

Exam Week   Week 18 to 19

Day 123 to 129 (7 Days)

This week is for writing your exam. We have put in seven days here just in case you need more time for review. By the end of these seven days you should have attempted the exam. This is the section that takes you from where you are to the next great level in your career.

The ICND1 and ICND2 exams are not easy in any way. You do have to work hard and earn your CCNA certification. It does not matter if you pass this on your first attempt or fifth. As soon as you pass **you will not be** a CCNA who passed on their fifth attempt. **You will be a CCNA**. No one cares how many attempts. All they care about is that you have passed this exam and can prove your understanding of the topics if asked in an interview.

Two Exam – MACH 2 Timeline

This timeline is for someone who was CCNA certified at one time or has attempted CCNA in the past 6 months. This is also for someone who has considerable experience in installing, maintaining and troubleshooting different network devices and just needs to learn to fill their knowledge gaps. For example, you may be familiar with RIP and OSPF but not with EIGRP. This is usually the case as any big network will use one or a maximum of two network protocols.

This time line has a faster pace than the first timeline. If you are reading this timeline directly without reading the first timeline we would suggest that you go over that at least once because there are many techniques that we have explained in the earlier timeline and do not want to repeat. As a matter of fact this time line is a condensed version of the first one so it is a good idea to read that as you may want to make your own timeline that is a hybrid between these two.

Another thing to note is that this timeline gives you weekly guidance only and gives you the freedom to make your own daily schedule. Reading the Mach 1 timeline will help you with the details of a daily schedule.

Note: *A day of study is 3 to 4 hours on a weekday and 8 or more hours on the weekend (about 36 hours per week).*

ICND1

Prep Time and Network Fundamentals

Day 1 to Day 7 (7 Days)

This is the week when you pick up your books gather your resources (refer to First timers timeline for a list of resources) to get ready for your express journey towards your CCNA certified status. Since this timeline is for someone who has attempted or was a CCNA. We assume that you already have a good understanding of topics like the OSI model, TCP/IP model etc. You are expected to finish your prep work and the network fundamentals topics in this week. This timeline is aggressive and is only a framework. You should modify this and make your own timeline that is best suited to you.

Sub-netting   Week 2 to 3

Day 8 to 16 (9 Days)

These nine days are dedicated for you to revise sub-netting. This is one of the most dreaded topics of CCNA and from personal experience if you have not used sub-netting in the past few months you will need to read this again. However you will be able to recover much faster and be confident in this topic. About 6 days of reading and watching VoD and about 3 days of hands on solving problems will get you to an exam ready status.

After these nine days you should be able to explain:

What are the different classes of Ipv4 Subnets?

Difference between Class-full and Class-less networks?

What is a subnet mask?

How to read and interpret a network with its subnet mask?

How to design a network with subnets given a requirement?

How to find the Broadcast Address, the Subnet Address and the number of hosts in a particular IP Address and subnet mask pair?

LAN Switching   Week 3 to 4

Days 17 to 27 (11 Days)

Continuing with this aggressive schedule we have put in 11 days for all the ICND1 switching topics. This may seem like too much to you if you remember the concepts from your earlier study and may need less time for this section. Perhaps you can just watch your VoD and do the labs and be done in a weeks' time. If you feel you need more time please refer to the first timeline for details.

Routing   Week 4 to 6

Day 28 to 38 (11 Days)

This section is dedicated to Routing. Believe me this was real fun section for me. I [Vivek] loved the concept of routing and how routers make life much easier and able to connect us globally. We are visual learners and we will recommend you to watch VoD and then do hands on labs. This is a quick way to revise your routing concepts and then doing labs will give you the confidence you need.

As stated earlier please do take you clues from the first timeline in case you are not able to decide how to divide studying for this section into a daily schedule.

WAN   Week 6 to 7

Day 39 to 47 (9 days)

This section relates to all the topics that are associated with connecting your LAN to another LAN that is in another city (like connecting the branch office to the main office) or connecting to the internet using your service provider. By the end of this section you should be able to know the various ways to connect to a WAN and do some basic troubleshooting on it. You should have an understanding of HDLC, PPP and should be able to configure these. Reading your book chapters thoroughly and watching the VoD will help you understand these topics. Hands on configuration and troubleshooting are highly recommended.

Final Section   Week 7 to 8

Day 48 to 54 (7 days)

This section is for you to sit down and revise all the topics especially the theoretical concepts. Start doing sample questions that came with your book, remember it is not good enough to get the answer correct you should also know the reason why it is so. It would be a good idea to go over each topic that Cisco expects you to know for the exam and see which ones need more work. See the VoD for those and read the relevant chapters in your book. Complete hands on labs where applicable but do this till you remove all doubts in your mind.

Exam time   **Week 8 and 9**

Day 55 to 61 (7 Days)

You should be taking the exam today or in the next six days. If you pass great you have moved ahead and have taken the first big step. In case you did not pass the exam don't worry it happens. Check you exam results sheet and see what your areas of weakness are and come right back and start hammering them out. Don't wait and don't get dis-heartened. Failure is a precursor to success, so don't let this stop you (See Chapter 33 "The Next Flight"). A few months from now when you are a CCNA you will not be remembering this small event of not passing the exam in your first attempt.

ICND 2

This starts your next big and final step towards you being a CCNA certified engineer.

ICND 2 is very technical and you have a lot to learn but this is real fun. You will see that all the technical concepts you learned in ICND 1 are being taken to the next level and more twists and turns are being added to them. Initially it may seem very complex but fear not as much of this can be done in hands on labs and that makes it much easier to understand. Anytime you feel overwhelmed refer back to the basics of that particular topic in your ICND 1 book.

Routing Protocols   **Week 1 to 3**

Day 1 to 16 (16 Days)

We will start ICND 2 preparation by going over routing protocols. You should be familiar with the concept of routing and may spend half a day on it and immediately start digging into one of the protocols. By the end of this section you should be comfortable with RIP, OSPF and EIGRP. It would be a good idea to prepare a table comparing the features of each of these protocols. This will give you clarity and will be a great aid to revise this topic. VoD and hands on labs will help you the most here and are strongly recommended.

By the time you finish this section you should be able to answer all the questions in your ICND2 book for the chapters related to this section.

IP Routing   **Week 3 to 4**

Day 17 to 26 (10 Days)

The next 26 days of your ICND2 journey are dedicated to other forms of Routing like the concepts of Static routing and how to control routing and flow of traffic by using Route summarization and Access Lists. We have all heard the phrase "One size fits all" and we also know that this approach does not always work. There are exceptions to the rule and it is the same for routing. There will be cases wherein you are required to route traffic for all devices from a datacenter to the internet except for a select few devices. Another example is that only these ten admin workstations are allowed to log on to network devices like routers and switches and five others are only allowed to log on to servers for administration. Sometimes critical traffic like voice for a call center uses a specific dedicated link while internet traffic will use another link. Whenever we have a situation like this access lists are used. Access Lists which are also called ACL's are of many different types and if not applied correctly can cause lot of problems. Adding or removing statements from an ACL is especially tricky so pay special attention to that while doing your hands on labs (It is a good idea to use notepad). That means that you should not only configure these but also learn to troubleshoot in case of a typo or any other errors. Needless to say VoD along with hands on labs will be needed to solidify the concepts and its uses in your mind.

Day 33 to 35 (3 Days)

After reading so much about the dynamic routing protocols you will learn that you can do without it by using static routes. However it is not practical to run a big network only on static routing. But this does not mean that it is not needed. Static routes are a part of any network.

Day 36 to 42 (7 Days)

These days are dedicated exclusively to different types of ACL's and how to use them. VoD and hands on lab is a must for this.

Day 43 to 50 (8 Days)

These days are dedicated to VLSM and route summarization. These concepts go hand in hand and your expertise of sub netting will help you here. Hands on labs are a must. Do watch VoD if any.

Day 51 to 58 (8 Days)

These days are here to cover any other topics related to Routing and to practice and perfect your knowledge of routing and different ways you can affect routing using ACL's, Route Summarization and static routes.

WAN   Week 4 to 7

Day 27 to 39 (13 Days)

Learning about routing and routing protocols leads to the topic of WAN. Frame relay is one of the topics that you will study in this section.

This was an integral part of WAN's but is slowly being overtaken by newer technologies. However this is still there even in the CCIE lab. Frame relay gives you a good learning base for WAN communications. We keep on hearing rumors that this topic will slowly be replaced by more relevant technologies. Cisco is in the forefront of technological development and it does a good job in keeping its Certifications updated but this also ensures that all Cisco Certified engineers will learn newer technologies because they will have to pass the exam to keep their certification current. All other WAN related topics like Point to Point links, VPN etc. are to be completely finished by the end of this section.

LAN Switching   **Week 7 to 8**

Day 40 to 49 (10 Days)

The first few weeks of your ICND2 journey are dedicated to routing. These three weeks are dedicated to LAN tasks. Hands on labs for this section makes you easily understand this topic.

Two major topics in LAN switching are VLAN's and Spanning tree. These are not only fundamental but also cool concepts and almost every network depends on these. Needless to say these are always a part of your ICND2 exam and any interview that you will attend. There will be more switching related topics like trunks, ether channel and port security and all those are to be covered in this section.

Lastly once you understand it and know how to configure it you should also know how to troubleshoot it. VoD will surely help you in spanning tree and there are many great Videos on YOUTUBE also by leading trainers on this topic.

IP Addressing   **Week 8 to 10**

Day 50 to 58 (9 Days)

Your journey of learning is nearing its end now. You have learned most of the technologies. All that is left is IP Addressing. Although you did quiet a bit about IP Addressing and sub-netting in ICND1 but ICND2 takes it a step further. This section addresses the problem with IP Address scaling using NAT or to use the latest and greatest IPv6. As of the publication of this book IPv6 is going towards a slow adoption and a good understanding of this will serve you for years to come. This section like any other section needs your full concentration and dedication to understand these topics.

As you come to the end of this section evaluate yourself. Depending on how comfortable you feel you should probably schedule your exam in the next 7 to 14 days.

Final Week   **Week 10 to 11**

Day 59 to 65 (7 Days)

This week is there for the exclusive purpose of revision and clearing up of any doubts if any. By the end of this week you should feel ready to take this exam. Practice and reread what you have learned. You will not only appreciate what you have learned but there may be doubts that will clear out in your mind as you bring together all the knowledge.

Try reading aloud or teaching a colleague any topics that you feel you are not at a hundred percent.

Exam Week   **Week 11 to 12**

Day 66 to 72 (7 Days)

This week is your exam week. We have put in a week here just in case you need more time for revision. By the end of this you should have attempted the exam. This is the section that takes you from what you are to the next great level in your career.

The ICND1 and ICND2 exams are not easy in any way. You do have to work hard and earn your CCNA certification, that is a given. But what does not matter is the amount of times it took you to pass the exam. As soon as you pass you will not be a CCNA who passed on their 5th attempt. You will be a CCNA, plain and simple. There is no need to worry that it took you x amount of attempts. Employers and organizations do not care how many attempts. They will not ask did you pass on your first attempt or your 5th attempt; the only thing they want to know is your technical knowledge, that you can prove your understanding of the topics and that you will be an asset to them.

One exam – Warp Speed Timeline

This final timeline is for someone who was a CCNA or has good experience in the networking field. You could fit into one or more of these situations:

- You are working for a Cisco partner and need to certify as a requirement for the partner.

- Maybe you have been working at a huge corporation and have been doing some part of networking for a few years and now need to move forward in your career.

- You have been managing network related projects for some time and want to be better at it by doing this certification.

- You are or have been a Unix administrator or server administrator and want to learn more networking

- Maybe you were a server administrator until now but because of server virtualization and blade servers you have to know networking also.

Basically this timeline is for someone who is familiar with networks, has access to network gear and network engineers and is in a hurry to be a CCNA.

There is a lot that has already been said in the first timeline so please do read that and then start following the timeline below. Of course you can modify this according to your requirements.

If you are someone new to networking and still want to the take just one exam then we advise you to combine the sections of ICND1 and ICND2 in the first timeline.

Since we have assumed you are already familiar with networking we are giving you a broad framework here. You can fill in the details using the first timeline in this Chapter.

Note: *A day of study is 3 to 4 hours on a weekday and 7 to 8 hours on the weekend (about 29 to 36 hours per week).*

Prep Time   Week 1

Day 1 to Day 7 (7 Days)

See two exam ICND1 time line for more details on preparation time.

Read, Watch VoD and do labs   Week 2 to 14

Day 8 to Day 98 (91 Days)

In these three months you can read your CCNA book from one end to the other or you can shuffle around by reading topics that you are more comfortable with. For example I ^(Vivek) would do a quick read of networking fundamentals may be 2 or 3 days to make sure that I pick up the terms and acronyms which may be asked in the test. Then I would go to my favorite IP Routing and Routing protocols. After watching the relevant VoD I will read the relevant chapters in the book. Only then will I actually try the hands on labs.

Remember to not only watch the VoD from your training provider and read the book but also refer to other sources of information like Videos on YouTube or any other websites. There are also many blogs and articles written by well-known trainers which will help you. Lastly an internet search for your queries will show you a lot of resources to read, so you will have to read them carefully to weed out any bad or out of date information. Always remember to check the date of information in the web because what was the standard in the year 2000 may have changed by now.

Once you are done with your favorite section, go to the rest of the sections using the same technique of watching, reading and doing labs.

Depending on your previous experience with networks and the number of hours you can dedicate you may be able to finish this in less than three months.

Boot Camp / Review   Week 15 to 17

Day 92 to Day 101 (10 Days)

Now is the time to take that boot camp. Taking this now will not only give you the chance to get all your questions answered but will also give you a chance to do labs with an instructor answering all your queries. The presence of an instructor is especially helpful when you are troubleshooting. On the other hand if you are not attending a boot camp you can use this time to review the technologies and do those hands on labs once again and perfect yourself so that you are ready to take your CCNA test.

Exam Week   **Week 17 to 18**

Day 102 to Day 108 (7 Days)

This is the week you have been working for so long. This is the week that will bring you closer to your dream. Yes this is the week you take your test and become a CCNA.

Just in case you did not pass we have allocated another two weeks for you to retake the exam (See chapter 33 "The next Flight").

CHAPTER 38: POLISH YOUR RESUME

It is time for your job search and to expand your career

After all the jubilation of being CCNA Certified and getting yourself what you had promised (see chapter 13 "Reward for your successful flight") it is time to use your knowledge.

Imagine this situation or actually visualize it. You started your journey some time ago. You had to put in hard work and at times struggled to learn and understand new technologies. You had to face setbacks and even failures at times but you persevered and have just acquired your CCNA certified status. You are victorious and you have conquered.

One of the primary reasons to attain CCNA for most engineers is to move forward in their careers.

CCNA is a very good career choice and as a result people of many different age groups from many different backgrounds study the CCNA course. We have seen people with 30 plus years of work experience to teenagers from high school take this certification. One thing is for sure they are all interested in networking. If you are one of those candidates, who want to move to a new job that is more aligned to your dream certification, or even want to move within your company, you will most probably have to create/update your resume and go on interviews. But are you fully prepared for career success?

The first step is creating an effective resume, always remember that a resume takes a lot of work and you have to put some time and effort into it. Here are four success strategies that we followed for our career search:

1) **Maintain focus** – A resume needs to be tailored to the specific industry and position. For this reason, it is not a good idea to use the same resume for every job that you are applying for. It is important to look at your resume from the prospective employer's point of view. When you change this view you are able to highlight the skills and experience which are most relevant for their needs. Employers don't care as much what you did before, compared to what you can do to help them today; and what relevant skills you bring to the table.

2) **Proofread carefully** – No matter how qualified you are or technically savvy one or two mistakes will give a negative impression to the employer. Employers will ask themselves if you will make the same mistakes on the job. Review your resume yourself multiple times, and then read the resume out loud, does it sound right? You should also have someone else, review your resume, even if they do not have any idea about specific technologies or equipment—they do know what sounds good and what doesn't.

3) **Keep it concise and specific** – The ability to communicate clearly and effectively is a skill sought by many employers and you can demonstrate your ability in this area through a carefully crafted resume. Maximum length for your resume is two pages, which should only include relevant experience

related to the position. You want to stand out from the crowd by demonstrating how you contributed to the organization.

4) **Presentation Counts** – Human resource personnel go through many resumes, so you want your resume to be pleasing and easy to read. You want to create a good impression so it is best to use a standard font such as Times New Roman. Don't get carried away and bold or italicize the entire resume, which can be very distracting. Try using bullet points rather than large paragraphs. Consistency in formatting is very important also so keep that in mind-don't change from bold to bullet points and back.

Keywords – The job description in the posting as well as the qualifications will likely provide you with many of the key words you will need to use. But keep in mind; don't just copy keywords from the job description or words that you are unsure of. The words should be relevant to the position you are applying for. You should also go to the company's website, check how they say things and what types of vocabulary they use. The goal is to get your resume noticed and move on to the interview portion. You see there is a big difference in having technical knowledge and understanding the technology. For example, we all know that every device on the network is given a hostname and you should know the command to set that. That is the technical knowledge. But distinguishing the fact that the hostname is also used for the following really shows you understand the technology.

- It is used for many tools and applications to access the device. For example telnet/ssh to the device

- The hostname also helps us when we run a trace route command in seeing the hops to a destination like 2doubleccie.com.

- The hostname along with other features can be used to authenticate a particular network device to be a part of the network.

Employers not only want to ensure you have the required technical knowledge, but they want to get a glimpse of your attitude, your goals and work ethic. Are you ready to jump in and finish the task on time? Do you take the necessary steps to go above and beyond? Can you ask questions and know when to escalate to superiors? Will you be a good investment? If so you will be chosen.

CHAPTER 39: PREPARATION FOR THE INTERVIEW

So you followed our advice in the previous chapter, and received that call you were waiting for, it is time for the interview. Here are some strategies that helped us.

1) **Research the company**

   You need to thoroughly research the potential company and get as much information as possible on its services, technologies, products, and customers/clients, where they are located, any awards etc. This preparation will definitely help you, not only get a better understanding of your perspective employer, but also show the employer you have done your homework. Don't underestimate the importance of being able to sell yourself by knowing your employer inside/out.

2) **Dress**

   First impressions are everything and your appearance will be the first thing the potential employer sees, dress correctly for the industry and the position you are entering into. Many networking companies do have a casual working environment, but you should not go to the interview dressed casually. When you are dressed professionally it shows, you are confident and you feel good. For example on the East coast of the U.S., you are expected to be dressed up more (no jeans or polo shirts) whereas in the Silicon

Valley you may wear more business casual attire to the interview. Please find out the company culture. If you can't find out from the website, just ask the human resources professional scheduling your interview.

3) **Preparation is key**

Take along extra copies of your resume, references, paper and pens to jot down notes. Most important is to prepare at the minimum three questions to ask at the end of the interview, try not to ask those clichéd or the usual questions about what is your timeline for hiring. When an employer states that this concludes the interview, the worst thing you can say is that you have no questions.

4) **Be prompt**

Ensure that you have the correct address for the interview and if the area is really new to you try and find the location beforehand. Get the correct address and allow some extra time for finding the place. Be there 10 to 15 minutes before the interview. Don't go earlier than 15 minutes since the employer may not be prepared and it also looks like you are extremely desperate.

5) **Be poised and self-confident**

- **Eye contact is the key** with the interviewers; but not staring them down.

- **Speak clearly** and **distinctly**.

- **A firm handshake** is important and says a lot to the employer (just be careful not to crush their hand especially if you are shaking hands with a lady)

6) **Be an alert listener**

You have to be on the ball and alert! Listen carefully to whatever is spoken. You have to also listen to read between the lines at what is not being said and how to pick up on this.

7) **Understand the question**

Many times during an interview the candidate does not understand the question, or cuts the interviewer off. Don't' be afraid to say, "Can you please repeat the question again?"

8) **Be precise & detailed**.

Always give concrete examples and speak about your accomplishments and what sets you apart from everyone. Be as specific as possible.

9) **Thank you note**

Once you have completed the interview you should send a note (via e-mail) within 24 hours to those responsible for interviewing you or the human resources professional who can pass it along. Never underestimate the power of a good thank you note; this enables you to stand out and keeps you fresh in the interviews mind. But ensure there are no spelling or grammatical errors and most important the names of interviewers are spelled correctly.

10) Follow up

Don't miss another opportunity to keep yourself on the company's radar. Many people don't follow up, but it is essential to either email, or call. This also helps you remind the interviewer of what you can do for their company.

For example in one session where Dean was interviewed for a position many years ago, the contract house informed him prior to meeting the customer to make sure to wear a suit and tie as one of the candidates failed to meet the management approval not because of his technical abilities, but rather to due to fact that in this company culture, the team would expect that all candidates are dressed appropriately for an interview with a proper attire. For that particular company and others the dress code means a lot and is a sign of respect for the position, for the company and as well as to the interviewers. That was a lesson learned by both the contract house and the first engineer that went for the earlier interview. The position paid well, and it could have secured a great opportunity which could have boosted his carrier, too bad he didn't read this book for this preparation. With that lesson in the back of Dean's mind, he began to do some research about the company, their business mode, their culture, their competition and the roles and responsibilities of the particular position. On the day of interview the contract house took Dean to the site. Here's the story from Dean's point of view:

The contract house sales rep and I drove together to the site for customer visit and interview. We arrived about fifteen minutes prior to the interview. During that time I keenly observed the company slogans and rewards displayed in the lobby. I was also in control and relaxed. I knew that if I went there fifteen minutes late, that interview wouldn't go well.

After a quick introduction, a firm hand shake and some small talk about the weather, it was time to interview. I listened attentively to the interviewer's questions and when I was ready to **answer I paused for a few seconds to make sure the interviewer was finished with his question and with these few seconds of silence all the attention was turned to me**. This allowed me to reflect on the question and to answer the specific content; this made the interviewers more curious as how the answers to their questions would be phrased. At various times the interviewers nodded and smiled. Once the technical portion of the interview was complete, the hiring manger asked some typical non-technical questions which would help them identify the personality type and to see if this person would be a good match for the team and for the company in general. These questions were similar to

- Give us an example of a situation where you failed.

- What was the situation and how did you resolve it?

For these type of questions, you can describe some technical problems, but the interviewer is looking for the various steps you took to resolve the situation, especially how you handle difficult situations, you need to be as detailed and methodical as possible and make sure to provide concrete examples.   Back to my interview, in brief, the session went very well, and the management team was impressed with my credentials and the manner with which I showed interest and respect to the interviewers and yet was still control of the interview session.   The position was offered right there and then.   The contract house was also very impressed with the entire process since they wanted this company's business for a while.

CONCLUSION

You are devoted enough to have purchased this guide book, which we believe is the first of its kind for CCNA enthusiasts, and have, hopefully, read all of the way to this point. Now it's time to take the test to pursue your CCNA certification.

We hope reading this book is just one of the many, steps you will take in this life changing journey. We believe that this pursuit of excellence has given you a strong work ethic, time management, team work, organizational and collaboration skills. By using many of these skills and practices mentioned in this book you will achieve greater success and career growth. The knowledge and belief in yourself that you have gained will propel you to bigger and better things.

It is our hope that we have, through this book, made a difference in your hunger, appetite and determination to go after and obtain your CCNA. Never listen to those that tell you it is too hard or not worth it. Only you, through hard work, perseverance, dedication, a positive attitude and determination, can feel the real joy in achieving a goal. That goal that at the beginning, seemed out of reach or even impossible by some naysayers will be achieved. Stay focused and strong, you can do it! In other words, you **are not going to sacrifice your long-term goals for short term gains.** Stay positive and don't ever give up. Remember, visualize—what you conceive in your mind, believe in your heart—and fulfill through your actions.

Let this book guide you towards a more fulfilling and happier road in your life journey, one where you will be CCNA certified.

We hope to hear from you and your success stories, which would be the greatest reward for the hard work we put into writing this book.

A Note from Dean & Vivek:

This guidebook is the sole effort of two fellow engineers like you, who dreamed of spreading what they learned in their quest for different certifications including two CCIEs.

If you like our advice and what we have written, then let your voice be heard globally by posting your comments on our facebook page.

Give us a review on Amazon and send an email to freebook@2doubleccies.com. We will send you our eBook "Your CCNA exam Success Strategy Learning by Immersing – Sink or Swim"
Thank You
www.2doubleccies.com

✓ Let us know how you feel about this book.
✓ Checkout our Videos
✓ Share your experiences. (contact@2doubleccies.com)
✓ Look for our Seminars and Webinars.

Books by Dean and Vivek.

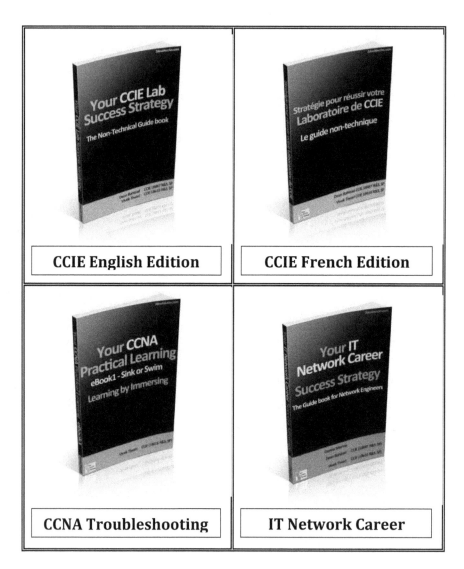

CCIE English Edition	**CCIE French Edition**
CCNA Troubleshooting	**IT Network Career**

www.ingramcontent.com/pod-product-compliance
Lightning Source LLC
LaVergne TN
LVHW022313060326
832902LV00020B/3434